# *Ars*
# EROTICA

# *Ars* EROTICA

## AN AROUSING HISTORY OF EROTIC ART

### EDWARD LUCIE~SMITH

**RIZZOLI**
NEW YORK

First published in the United States of America in 1997 by

Rizzoli International Publications Inc.

300 Park Avenue South, New York, NY, 10010

ISBN 0-8478-5781-6

LC 97-67799

This book was conceived, designed and produced by

The Ivy Press Limited

2/3 St. Andrews Place

Lewes, East Sussex

BN7 1UP

Art Director: Peter Bridgewater

Designer and page layout: Sara Nunan

Commissioning Editor: Viv Croot

Managing Editor: Anne Townley

Editor: Vicki Harrison

Picture research: Liz Eddison

Printed and bound in Singapore

Cover illustration: Eric Gill, *Female Nude, Lying*, 1937

# Contents

SEX *in the* HEAD
Page 6

*Naked as* ADAM
Page 20

*Naked as* EVE
Page 36

*Loves of the* GODS
Page 56

*Down to* EARTH
Page 72

LOOKING *on*
Page 94

*Boys will be* BOYS
Page 106

*Women* IN LOVE
Page 118

*En plein* AIR
Page 130

*Solitary* PLEASURES
Page 148

*Coming* TOGETHER
Page 160

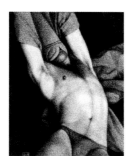

*All* CHANGE
Page 170

*Love* HURTS
Page 180

*Index of Artists*
Page 190

*Acknowledgements*
Page 192

# SEX *in the* HEAD

ABOVE: *This 1793 illustration, by an anonymous artist, comes from* Thérèse philosophe ou Memoires, *a novel written during the French Revolution. The orgy it depicts is paradoxically decorous.*

IF BEAUTY IS IN THE EYE OF THE BEHOLDER, *eroticism is in his or her mind. It is not merely what we look at or read but how we perceive it which governs our reactions. Does the image or text stimulate us? Does it offend us? Does it do both of these things simultaneously? From at least the sixteenth century onwards, Western culture offers a long history of official attempts to suppress the erotic. The result has been a continuous series of causes célèbres, ranging from the Giulio Romano / Pietro Aretino series* I Modi *published in the early sixteenth century to the Robert Mapplethorpe trial in 1990.*

*Since* I Modi *— better known in English as 'Aretine's Attitudes' — are now not as accessible as Mapplethorpe's much reproduced photographs, as nearly all the original prints have perished, it is worth saying something about them here. They consisted of a series of designs illustrating various positions for heterosexual intercourse. These were drawn c.1524 by Giulio Romano (1499–1546), Raphael's chief assistant, engraved by Marcantonio Raimondi (c.1480?–1534), responsible for reproducing many of Raphael's own compositions, and accompanied by a series of poems by the scapegrace satirist and propagandist Pietro Aretino (1492–1557). The collection caused an uproar in papal Rome and all three perpetrators had to flee.*

*Giulio Romano took refuge in Mantua, where the ruling duke was only too happy to employ such an eminent artist. Raimondi, less fortunate, was imprisoned for a while by an enraged Pope Clement VII. Aretino fled to Venice, and from this safe haven conducted a profitable business in literary blackmail (offering to suppress his own satires in return for suitable amounts of cash). The prints themselves were destroyed wherever the puritanically inclined found them, and now survive chiefly in the form of a crude series of woodcut copies, rediscovered only in 1928 after coming into the possession of Walter Toscanini, book-collecting son of the great conductor Arturo Toscanini.*

' *If after death it were decent to be had, I'd say: Let's fuck, let's fuck so much we die; There we'll all fuck — you, Adam, Eve, and I — For they invented death and thought it bad.* '

PIETRO ARETINO
*1492–1557*
LET'S FUCK, DEAR HEART

*Though little aesthetic pleasure is to be had from these copies, they do demonstrate the fact that Giulio Romano based himself on Greek and Roman precedents. His designs are indebted to the erotic frescoes by classical artists then beginning to be discovered in Rome through the excavation of the buried imperial palaces such as Nero's Golden House. Aretino's poems, on the other hand, show that descriptions and representations of sexual acts necessarily continued to be viewed through the complex prism of the Judaeo-Christian tradition. There is a third thread which links these two others: it is fairly clear that I Modi are also a satire on the papal court, and represent some of the leading courtesans of the day, each identifiable through a particular sexual speciality, with their noble lovers.[1] Contemporary readers would know who was who also.*

*All of these elements reappear in later erotic art and literature, or at least in that part of it which is linked to the Western tradition. Erotic works are often a number of things simultaneously: hedonistic, guilt-ridden, boldly critical of society, and transgressive for transgression's sake. Usually they combine at least two of these four elements.*

*If one looks at the progression of erotic art in the West, it is possible to discern a number of turning points. Two of these occur in the eighteenth century. One is predicated on a single event – the rediscovery of the lost Roman cities of Pompeii and Herculaneum. These discoveries, made from 1748 onwards, revived the interest in Roman fresco painting which had affected the generation of Raphael and Giulio Romano. At the same time, they were a considerable cultural shock. Antiquity was visible for the first time in its everyday completeness. The multitude of erotic representations discovered in the two buried cities presented the educated class of the time with a cultural dilemma – not least because their education was still largely founded on the study of classical texts. How were these images to be absorbed into the idealized picture of the classical world passed on to them by their schoolmasters, who had skilfully steered their pupils past the erotic passages to be found in admired classical authors such as Catullus and Ovid?*

*The solution was never formulated in so many words, but a consensus formed that these images must be set apart and made available only to the mature and sophisticated. The sexual commonplaces of Roman life were sequestered in the notorious Secret Museum in Naples, viewable on payment of a fee, and available only to males. Some modern theorists have put forward the idea that the modern notion of 'pornography' has its roots in these Pompeian discoveries, and specifically in the search for a way to deal with and neutralize them without wholly denying their existence.*

---

1. See *I Modi*, a cura di Lynne Lawner (Longanesi & Co., Milan, 1984) pp. 31–5.

### Let's Fuck, Dear Heart

(Sonetti Lussuriosi 9)

' Let's fuck, dear heart, let's have it in and out,
For we're obliged to fuck for being born,
And as I crave for cunt, you ache for horn,
Because the world would not make sense without.

If after death it were decent to be had,
I'd say: Let's fuck, let's fuck so much we die;
There we'll all fuck – you, Adam, Eve, and I –
For they invented death and thought it bad.

Really it's true that if those first two thieves
Had never eaten that perfidious fruit,
We'd still know how to fuck (though not wear leaves).

But no more gossip now; let's aim and shoot
The prick right to the heart, and make the soul
Burst as it dies in concert with the root.

And could your generous hole
Take in as witnesses these bobbing buoys
For inside testimony of our joys? '

PIETRO ARETINO
1492–1557

*The other eighteenth-century turning-point occurred in France, and was the product of the struggle between the representatives of the Enlightenment, and eventually those of the French Revolution, and those of the* ancien régime. *This struggle was never simple, and where the treatment of sex and sexuality was concerned, it created paradoxes of a sort which continue to bedevil us today. On the one hand the* philosophes, *the representatives of the Enlightenment, liked to present themselves as the champions of a new and purer way of living, opposed to the corruption of the court. This is the role which Denis Diderot takes up in his Salons – critical commentaries on the nine official exhibitions put on between 1759 and 1781. Diderot maintained that our idea of beauty arose from the emotions as much as from the intellect, that it came from the 'conformity of the imagination with the object'. In practical terms, he supported the bourgeois, moralizing art of Jean-Baptiste Greuze (1725–1805) against the frivolous inventions of the Mme de Pompadour's favourite, François Boucher (1703–70).*

*The contrast between the two painters is not, however, as simple as Boucher's formulations might suggest. Boucher is indeed an erotically charged artist, and his eroticism spills over from mythological scenes into representations of contemporary life which were certainly designed to titillate the spectator. One can, however, argue that Boucher's eroticism is of a much healthier variety than that which surfaces in many paintings by his rival. Greuze alternated moralizing genre-scenes, such as* The Return of the Prodigal Son *(c. 1765), with slightly prurient representations of pubescent girls, each with some attribute which suggests innocence either endangered, or actually lost (*The Broken Jug*). The atmosphere of these paintings by Greuze is exactly that of much of the libertine literature of the time, and it is worth remembering that some of these libertine authors, notably Mirabeau, were to become leaders of the Revolution itself.*

*In fact the more closely one studies this body of literature, the more obvious it becomes that it was written not simply to entertain but as a way of criticizing and undermining a social system which seemed increasingly intolerable. The crudest examples are the anonymous tracts, sometimes provided with graphic illustrations, which accuse Marie-Antoinette of lesbianism, citing the ill-fated*

BELOW: *Japanese artist* **Foujita** *(1886–1968) worked in Paris for many years. The oriental element of* Couple nu Enlacé *of 1932 adds to the erotic piquancy of the image.*

LEFT: In **Jacopo Tintoretto's** Woman Baring Her Breasts *the breasts belong to a sixteenth-century Venetian courtesan. Such Venetian generosity was widely reported by worldy travellers.*

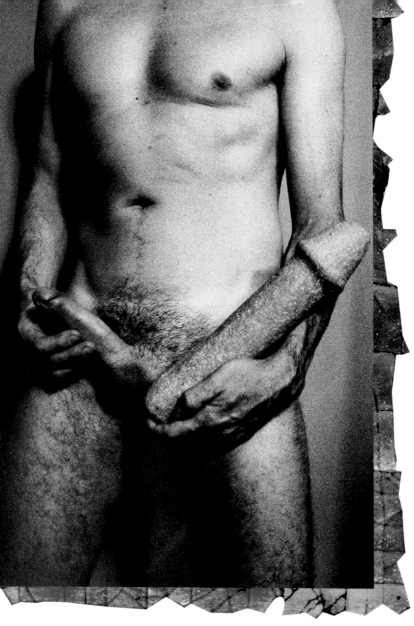

Princesse de Lamballe as her partner. The most telling denunciation of the society of the time, itself charged with erotic atmosphere, is Pierre Choderlos de Laclos' epistolary novel Les Liaisons Dangereuses, (1782), recently the basis for a play by Christopher Hampton and two films.

Yet Laclos is not the most controversial author of the period. That honour belongs to the Marquis de Sade (1740–1814), whom the French intellectuals connected with the Surrealist Movement and later elevated to the status of culture hero. Born in 1740, de Sade was several generations younger than Diderot, and his background was a great deal grander. On his mother's side he was related to a junior branch of the French royal house. His youth and young manhood were marked by a series of increasingly serious sexual scrapes, involving violence towards women. In 1777 his vengeful mother-in-law had him arrested under a lettre de cachet. It was in these unpropitious circumstances that his new life as a writer began.

De Sade's most celebrated works, The New Justine and Juliette, belong to the intellectual climate of the French Revolution, though they also show traces of the influence of earlier libertine writers such as Prévost, Crébillon and Restif de la Bretonne. Released in April 1790, after periods in the Château de Vincennes, the Bastille and the asylum at

ABOVE: In **Edward Lucie-Smith's** Untitled 1997 photograph, the sexuality of the model is emphasized by the cropping of his head and shoulders, directing attention to the marble Sino-Siberian penis votive, dating from about 1000 BC, that he carries.

Charenton, Sade, despite his aristocratic background, now saw himself as an obvious victim of the regime which had just fallen. Others did not necessarily agree. Accused of royalist sympathies, he was imprisoned yet again in 1793–94, and only just escaped with his life. In this period of turmoil he was nevertheless able to arrange for the clandestine publication of his two novels. Their notoriety cost him the liberty he had precariously regained. Napoleon, now First Consul and busy trying to clean up the moral chaos left behind by the Reign of Terror and its corrupt successor the Directory, saw him as an obvious target. He was re-arrested in 1801, and finally ended his days in 1814, back at Charenton.

Justine and Juliette remain controversial works today, though de Sade has been elevated to the pantheon of great French writers. A complete, official, non-clandestine edition of his works began to be issued in 1986. His writing retains much of its force, as a considered act of social, religious and sexual iconoclasm, yet even today many of those who admit de Sade's importance are made profoundly uncomfortable by the savage violence of his imagination. Nevertheless in a certain sense he remains isolated historically. There are no independent works of visual art from his period which transgress in the same way, and the illustrations added to some editions of his novels are without aesthetic merit.

*The nineteenth century saw several more turns of the wheel in the development of the Western erotic sensibility. Indeed, it is probably true to say that, despite profound social and intellectual changes, the attitudes of a large part of the contemporary audience still have nineteenth-century roots. Basically there are two narratives in the eroticism of the period. One deals in romantic fantasy. This may take several forms, but one of the commonest is that of the oriental daydream, copiously represented in the art of the period, from the time of Ingres (1780–1867) and Delacroix (1798–1863) onwards, and certainly not absent from its fiction. The other, and in the end more important, is realism – the representation of everyday life. It was realistic erotic paintings and narratives which caused the authorities of the period their great degree of perturbation. Hence, for example, the unsuccessful prosecution of Flaubert's novel* Mme Bovary *(1857), and the uproar occasioned by Manet's* Olympia *(1865) and his* Déjeuner sur l'herbe *(1863).*

*There is a significant difference at this period between literary and artistic culture in France and their equivalents on the other side of the Channel. English Victorians often saw French culture as inherently loose and immoral, and material which was freely published in France, such as the realistic novels of Zola, attracted prosecutions for obscenity when imported to England. Henry Vitzelly was imprisoned in 1889 for publishing English translations. The distinction between what was mainstream and what was clandestine or forbidden seems to have been much more firmly and clearly drawn among the British at this period than among the French. The erotic impulse in Britain was primarily literary, not artistic – or perhaps one could say that the erotic impulse, here chiefly typified by an interest in the female nude, was still able to find socially acceptable channels for itself. Many such nudes appeared in the Royal Academy exhibitions every year, just as they did in the Paris Salons, but contextualized in such a way that the middle-class public did not find them offensive.*

*In literature the situation was different. Alongside the Victorian 'classics' – Dickens, Thackeray, George Eliot, Trollope, Thomas Hardy – we find a series of erotic narratives unabashedly designed to arouse, which unlike those published in France before the Revolution, profess no serious philosophical, social or ethical aim. Nevertheless they are often of great psychological and sociological interest. Among these books are* Venus in India, *by 'Captain Charles Devereaux', and the anonymous* First Training *and* The Adventures of Lady Harpur. *The first of these is set at the time of the First Afghan War (1840). The other two belong to the 1880s. In all three of these titillating works, the*

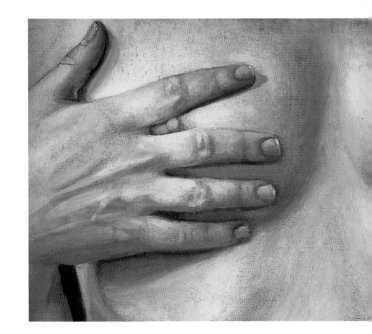

*characterization emphasizes the idea of women as independent personalities, pursuing their own satisfaction, and scornful of sexual hypocrisy. This is not Victorian society – repressed, polite and repelled by sex – as it is normally presented to us.*

*The great English erotic classic of the period is the massive* My Secret Life *by 'Walter' (c.1888), a highly detailed, multi-volume record of one man's sexual odyssey. Walter has sometimes been identified with the bibliophile Henry Spencer Ashbee (1834–1900), who compiled the first major English bibliography of erotic and pornographic writing, the* Index Librorum Prohibitorum, *published in 1877. But the facts do not seem to fit. Many indications in the text suggest that Walter belonged to an earlier generation, and may have been born somewhere in the second decade of the century.* My Secret Life *presents itself as fact not fiction, and, despite the enormous number of encounters it records, this claim seems to be convincing.*

The book offers a candid and totally unvarnished panorama of Victorian sexual life, as seen through the eyes of a man of unbounded erotic appetites. Originally published in a very limited edition, it did not become generally available, even in clandestine form, until the beginning of the twentieth century. The first complete commercial edition appeared in Paris in 1902.

By the time this was available, the phenomenon of fin de siècle decadence was already sputtering to an end, and the first rumblings of the Modern Movement had begun to be heard. Decadence had first made itself felt, in Britain at least, in the poems of Algernon Charles Swinburne; and was fully manifest in aspects of Oscar Wilde, most notably perhaps in his play Salome (1893) and in his novella The Picture of Dorian Gray (1891); and in the illustrations of Aubrey Beardsley and his prose narrative Under the Hill (1903). With the fin de siècle, sexual allusion, and sometimes direct sexual confrontation, became a weapon of the artist or writer who wished to seem 'advanced'.

In France, then a much more tolerant society, artists and writers had to take even stronger measures if they wished to challenge the complacency of their audience. It is worth comparing, for example, the fantasy of Beardsley's illustrations to the Lysistrata (1896) of Aristophanes with the sardonic realism of Lautrec's series of lithographs Elles, which take the spectator behind the scenes in the world of Parisian brothels, with particular emphasis on the lesbian relationships between the prostitutes who worked in these establishments.

BELOW: In L'Entremetteuse, **Cesare Dandini** depicts a familiar seventeenth-century Florentine scene: a madame offering a girl to a client.

Lautrec (1864–1901) could look back to Degas (1834–1917) as his exemplar, in particular to a series of monotypes made by Degas as illustrations to de Maupassant's La Maison Tellier (1881). He also anticipated the climate of fully developed Modernism, since he was a principal influence on the Picasso of the Blue and Rose periods. Sexuality remained a driving force in Picasso's work throughout his long career. Les Demoiselles d'Avignon (1907), a crucial turning-point in the evolution of Cubism, also shows a scene in a brothel – one of a much more sordid kind than those which Lautrec had frequented. Apollinaire (1880 –1918), one of Picasso's closest associates in the pre-1914 period when Modernism was created, earned part of his living as a writer of pornographic books.

The emphasis on sexuality in early modern art could be turned in one of two directions. In the hands of the German Expressionists, and still more so in those of their successors, the harsh realists of the Neue Sachlichkeit (New Objectivity), it became an instrument of social criticism. Immediately after World War I artists such as George Grosz and Otto Dix used sexual representations to satirize those who, despite Germany's crushing defeat, seemed to have 'done well out of the war'. Their images express both fascination and disgust with the corrupt society of the Weimar Republic.

In Paris, the Surrealist Movement, founded by André Breton (1896–1966) and his associates in 1924, saw sexuality as the irresistible force which would shatter the established conventions of bourgeois society. That is, the discoveries of Freud were to be brought to the aid of Marx. Surrealist art, especially in the hands of Salvador Dalí (1904–89), felt free to express the wildest sexual fantasies.

The explosive nature of the materials the surrealists made use of were illustrated by some of the schisms within the Movement itself. Dalí has, since his death in 1989, been identified by a number of writers on his work as a deeply closeted homosexual, who used his publicly proclaimed submission to his formidable wife Gala as a way of concealing his true desires from others, and perhaps even from himself. Yet Dalí also and quite consciously employed half-concealed homosexual imagery as a means of provoking Breton, whose claims to total control of the Surrealist group he resented. Breton, for all his self-proclaimed faith in the total liberation of the psyche, was quite unable to deal with the idea of sexual relationships between males. Another artist who made use of sexual teasing of this sort was Marcel Duchamp (1887–1968), who on occasion adopted the pseudonym 'Rose Sélavy', a pun on the French phrase 'Rose, c'est la vie', and had himself photographed wearing elegant female attire.

The battles over censorship fought from the 1920s to the beginning of the 1960s, which encompass such celebrated conflicts with the British and American legal systems as the prosecutions brought against James Joyce's Ulysses (1922) and D.H. Lawrence's Lady Chatterley's Lover (1928), have created the climate in which erotic material, both old and new, is usually examined today. The received opinion is that the climate, in English-speaking countries at least and also in most parts of Western Europe, is one of almost complete permissiveness, or where almost anything of a sexual nature can be said, written, represented in visual images or published. This permissiveness, in turn, is usually associated with a generally libertarian, left-leaning political and social climate.

It does not take much examination to discover that these propositions are in many respects of doubtful validity today in the 1990s. The Pop Art

BELOW: The partial concealment of the model's face in this half-length female nude enables spectators to project their emotions on to the figure, making her a more flexible subject for fantasy.

RIGHT: *One of* **Andres Serrano's** *ironic nudes from* A History of Sex, *1997; posed against a flat Dutch landscape, she pays homage to innumerable downmarket pin-ups.*

of the 1960s is still usually seen as something which summarizes, through its choice and use of imagery, the increasingly relaxed sexual attitudes which were becoming prevalent in Western society. Pop prided itself on its deep roots in mass culture – that is, in the tastes and preferences of the urban blue-collar majority. One of the things it borrowed most eagerly from this culture was the pin-up – the image of the nubile, scantily clothed or totally unclothed young woman, whose identity as an individual was lost in her more general function as an object of male sexual desire. Some of the most candid statements about the cultural function of the pin-up were made in the American painter Tom Wesselman's series of **Great American Nudes**, *images where the facial features of the model are largely obliterated, while her sexual signifiers – mouth, nipples and often vagina – are emphasized.*

Today, images of this type – and indeed the whole culture of the pin-up – of the female as the passively receptive object of the masculine gaze, are often fiercely condemned by people who would in other respects characterize themselves as politically and socially liberal.

It seems likely that the 1970s and 1980s will be seen by posterity as an epoch in which ideas about sexuality, and therefore about erotic texts and representations, fell into a condition of chaos unknown perhaps since the turbulent beginning of the Christian era. What seems at first sight like the continued growth of permissiveness appears, at a second or third glance, to be something more closely resembling a radical re-alignment of frontiers. In Western society we are now more tolerant and accepting of some things, and increasingly intolerant of others. Meanwhile Eastern societies – India, China and the Islamic world – which have their own strongly entrenched erotic traditions – are visibly less permissive in the late twentieth century than they have been in the past. No popular Indian movie, for example, would dare to offer anything remotely resembling the erotic contortions to be seen carved on the great medieval temple at Khajuraho.

In the West, many factors have been at work. One is the rise of feminism. Though feminist doctrine is not a unity, many feminists stress the need for equality of sexual satisfaction and, as a logical consequence of that, acknowledge, and even encourage, equality of desire. One result of this has been a much increased production of erotic work both by women and, in many but not all cases,

BELOW: **Antonia Deutsch's** *back view of a female nude demonstrates the way in which contemporary photographers continue to quote Old Master paintings: in this case, an Ingres Odalisque.*

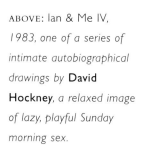

addressed to women. Erotic works of visual art, like the example by the leading feminist artist Judy Chicago (born 1939), are, however, still much rarer than erotic texts written by females from a female point of view. Some large British mainstream bookstores now keep a small section labelled 'Herotica'. It is noticeable that a good deal, though certainly not all, of this new erotic writing by women deals with lesbian encounters. 'Herotica' has also found its way on to the shelves of some public libraries: a situation unthinkable even 15 years ago.

Lesbianism, like male homosexuality, has during the past two decades gradually moved into the cultural mainstream. Homosexual erotic texts, often extremely forthright in their descriptions of physical acts, are also stocked by mainstream bookstores in Britain. In the United States, the situation seems to be rather different. Here, such books are to be found primarily in 'gay' bookstores. Most areas of the USA nevertheless show a greater tolerance of gay male pictorial erotica than is the

ABOVE: Ian & Me IV, 1983, one of a series of intimate autobiographical drawings by **David Hockney**, a relaxed image of lazy, playful Sunday morning sex.

case in Britain, though in Britain the situation appears to be changing rapidly. The increased tolerance of sexual deviation is clearly linked to the new respect for minority cultures of all kinds which is now such a feature of British, and even more so, of American society. The situation with regard to heterosexual erotica is rather different. Erotic texts, of a kind still recently strictly forbidden, have become freely available over the counter.

Despite this apparent liberalization, there is still continuing pressure from a section of the feminist movement to have erotic texts and, more so, erotic visual representations of women banned. The demand first made itself heard in the United States in the mid 1970s, that is in the aftermath of the Vietnam War. The feminist organization Women Against Rape was founded in 1976. This event was immediately preceded by the publication of Susan Brownmiller's book Against Our Will: Men, Women and Rape, which appeared in 1975 and which still remains one of the most cogent statements of this particular position. For Brownmiller, and those who agree with her, the representation of the naked female is an act of rape – the gaze, specifically the male gaze, is as brutally invasive as an actual penis.

LEFT: **Henri de Toulouse-Lautrec** frequently resided in some of the great Parisian brothels. Two Friends (c. 1896) reveals his fascination with the lesbian activity which went on behind the scenes.

*Brownmiller's argument against erotic representations is summarized thus:*

' Pornography, like rape, is a male invention, designed to dehumanise women, to reduce the female
to an object of sexual access...The staple of porn will always be the naked female body, breasts and
genitals exposed, because, as man devised it, her naked body is the female's 'shame', her private parts the
private property of a man, while his are the ancient, holy, universal, patriarchal instrument of his power,
his rule by force over her. '

*In 1993, when on a lecture-tour of New Zealand sponsored by the Arts Council of New Zealand,
I was asked to give an extra seminar at a leading university – one whose written constitution
guarantees both freedom of expression and the free exchange of information. The subject was impeccably
academic – the transformation of the nude in the switch from the Rococo style in France to
Neo-Classicism. On arrival, I was informed that the seminar had been cancelled, due to the objections
of a feminist member of the art-history department. Her reason was that my slide presentation would
inevitably include naked females (depicted by the likes of Antoine Watteau (1684–1721) and Jacques-
Louis David (1748–1835)), and that this was no longer permissible. More interesting than the objection
itself was the fact that the university authorities immediately accepted it, without entering into debate.*

*The real crux of the argument, however, lies in the relationship
between eroticism and photography. On this subject it is worth
quoting Susan Sontag's famous essay* On Photography
*(1976) at some length:*

' Photographs really are experience captured, and the camera is the
ideal arm of consciousness in its acquisitive mood.

To photograph is to appropriate the thing being photographed.
It means putting oneself into a certain relationship with the world
that feels like knowledge – and, therefore, like power. A now
notorious first fall into alienation, habituating people to abstract the
world into printed words, is supposed to have engendered that
surplus of Faustian energy and psychic damage needed to build
modern, inorganic societies. But print seems a less treacherous form
of leaching out the world, of turning it into a mental object, than
photographic images, which now provide most of the knowledge
people have about the look of the past and the reach of the present,
What is written about an event is frankly an interpretation, as are
handmade visual statements, like paintings or drawings.

Photographed images do not seem to be statements about the
world so much as pieces of it, miniatures of reality that anyone can
make or acquire. '[2]

*The literal truth of some of Sontag's observations has been
undermined during the two decades since her book was
published by the rapid growth of digitization, which makes the
photographic image a fluid rather than a fixed entity. Yet her
words retain an indisputable authority. This is how we*

BELOW: **Arthur Tress** *is
famed for his slightly
surreal photographs of
men.* Superman Fantasy
*of 1978 offers an ironic
commentary on the
popular myth of
male potency.*

**2**. Susan Sontag, *On Photography* (Allen Lane, London, 1978) pp. 3–4.

*continue to see photographs, even though we know that they can now be inventions or constructs, just as much as any other form of visual art. It is also easy to perceive the link between Sontag's theory and what Susan Brownmiller has to say. For both, the photographic image is an instrument of power, with an influence over sexuality now ceded to no other form of visual representation.*

*This is implicitly conceded in the work of a number of leading transgressive artists of the 1980s and 1990s. The images Jeff Koons (born 1953) made of himself in sexual congress with his then wife, the Italian porn-star and politician La Cicciolina and, more recently, a series of sexual images made by Andres Serrano as part of a commission from the Groningen Museum in Holland owe their effect to the fact that they are photographic representations, not drawn or painted ones. Furthermore, they are images which offer an ironic homage to the visual conventions of popular adult magazines. It seems likely that without the context supplied both by these and by the feminist campaign against such materials, they would lose nearly all of their impact.*

*If photographs of nude women have attracted hostile attention in the past two decades, this is still more the case with images which touch on the increasingly thorny topic of child sexuality and adult sexual response to children. One problem with contemporary culture is its increasing inability to divorce the state of nudity from the act of sex, something which the artists of earlier epochs were certainly capable of doing.*

*Renaissance art inherited from antiquity the image of the naked child, first as a personification of Eros, and secondly (there is a slight contradiction here) as a personification of innocence. There are numerous paintings and large decorative schemes, dating from the fifteenth to the eighteenth centuries, in which these nude children play a prominent part. It is only occasionally that we are aware of a sexual frisson. Donatello's bronze* David, *with its coquettish stance, is perhaps a case in point. We know from literary sources that Donatello was homosexual, and the sculpture seems to speak of a personal attraction to pubescent boys, as does at least one celebrated later work – Caravaggio's (1571–1610)* Amore Vincitore *in Berlin, where a naked and obviously knowing street urchin presides over a heap of symbolic objects. The effect of these masterpieces is nevertheless so complex, both culturally and emotionally, and they are so integral to the story of Western art, that no one has yet proposed that they be banished from sight.*

*In the eighteenth century, especially in France, there was a change of emphasis. It became fashionable to show children, often naked, engaged in versions of adult occupations and pursuits. Often the children are shown kissing or embracing. There are two strands here – one harmless, one less so. An aspect of the Rococo was its jesting trivialization both of the solemnities of mythology and the drudgery of the everyday world. Rococo pictures of naked children suggest that everything, myth and fact, can be homogenized as the materials for a harmless frolic. Nothing, these pictures and sculptures tell us, is to be taken too seriously. Yet the fact that the children behave in a 'grown-up' way undoubtedly adds an element of eroticism, deliberately cultivated by the artists and relished by their original audience.*

*The Rococo period in France lies on the cusp of a profound change in attitudes towards childhood in general. This was largely brought about by the writings of Jean-Jacques Rousseau (1712–78) (who abandoned his own children in orphanages where, given the condition of such institutions at the time, they died more likely than not without reaching maturity). Essentially what Rousseau did was to take the Christian idea of Original Sin and turn it on its head. In his idealized universe, children became the vessels of everything that was pure and true, and were later corrupted by experience of the world.*

*This is the situation which has now been complicated both by the explorations of Freud, which demonstrated how early sexual feeling manifests itself, and how profoundly sexual feelings in extreme youth shape the rest of our lives, and also by the intervention of the camera. Today photographic images of children which are made with sexual intent, or which, though not so made, nevertheless excite sexual feeling in some spectators, seem threatening. Though we know children do have sexual impulses, we prefer not to be brutally confronted with evidence of these. We cannot, despite our familiarity with Freudian concepts, deal with the idea that parental love or its surrogates may contain a sexual element.*

*I here return to the point with which I began: that eroticism lies, not in the written word, not in drawn, painted or sculptured representations, and not in photographs — that is, not in any of the things which are actually to be found in the pages of this book — but in the mind of the beholder. For this reason alone attempts to control the production and consumption of erotic literature and art are bound to fail. Indeed, to some extent at least, they always have failed. If Giulio Romano's elegant erotic engravings were suppressed, we still possess the crude woodcut copies of them.*

*In the present decade the situation has been enormously reinforced by the proliferation of the new electronic culture. Anyone with even the most superficial acquaintance with the Internet knows the gigantic amount of erotic material it makes available to anyone who has the use of a personal computer. And anyone who knows anything about personal computers will be aware that there is essentially no way to make this information inaccessible. As soon as some form of barrier is erected, a computer hacker will pull it down.*

*The sexual drive is admitted, even by those who deplore its effects, to be the most powerful of human impulses. It may well be that certain types of erotica ought to be vigorously discouraged. Yet even that discouragement is inevitably going to fall short of total suppression. As for the rest, erotic art and literature have much to tell us about our own nature as human beings, much to tell us about the actual context in which we live, and much to please the aesthetic sense. We may shut our eyes and close our ears, but they are not going to go away. Eroticism is inextricably part of the fabric of the contemporary world.*

BELOW: **Chris Nelson's**
*Duke of 1989 comes from his influential collection of pictures The Bear Cult. During the 1980s, the San Francisco photographer was one of those responsible for creating a new rugged and hirsute image for gay men.*

RIGHT: *A powerful study,*
Half-length Male Nude, *by*
**Théodore Géricault**
*(1791–1824), painted for a
student competition at the
Académie des Beaux Arts;
the picture once belonged
to Rudolf Nureyev.*

# Naked as
# ADAM

*t*he nude male body plays a central role in western culture – something which cannot be said of any other civilization. At the same time, this role is an extremely ambiguous one, carrying with it connotations that mingle pride, exhibitionism and shame. One reason for this ambiguity is the conflict between the Judaeo-Christian and the pagan traditions. The emphasis on male nudity comes to us from the Greeks, and after the Greeks from the Romans. Shame, and the prohibition of nudity, in particular of any exposure of a man's private parts, are inherited from the monotheistic religions of the Ancient Near East, Judaism in particular, and were further reinforced by the early Christian reaction that emerged against pagan practices.

The Greeks were not the inventors of totally unclothed male statues. These occur occasionally in Ancient Egyptian art, generally as surrogates for the embalmed body of the ruler, in case this should be destroyed through accident or malice. Such statues were part of tomb furniture, and never intended for public display. In addition to these, the Egyptians made representations of the fertility god Min. In this case, the statue itself tended to be rather rough and stylized, with a large erect phallus that was carved as a separate piece, and inserted into a hole in the torso. The Greeks seem to have been the first to make representations of naked youths as images of ideal beauty. These *kouroi*, as they were called, were not cult statues but dedications or offerings at the shrine of a god. Male gods, too, were depicted in a state of nudity – as mature men, in the case

*'... square and trim he stood breathing heavily and luxuriating under the water before turning his back and loosening his glittering briefs to reveal a firm hairless ass, milky white between the sun or sunbed-tanned zones of his back and thighs.'*

ALAN HOLLINGHURST
THE SWIMMING POOL LIBRARY 1988

of Zeus, the ruler of the gods, and his brother the sea-god Poseidon, but also as beings just blossoming into manhood. This was the form chosen for representations of the sun-god, Apollo, and the wine-god, Dionysus.

The Greeks also depicted male nudity in scenes taken from everyday life – athletes in competition were shown nude, so were the participants in symposia or drinking parties. These depictions survive, not as wall paintings, which are almost entirely lost, but on numerous black and red figure vases. Part of a flourishing export trade based on Athens, these vases have been excavated all over the Greek world, and vast quantities of them have been found in cemeteries in Etruria.

The emphasis on the male in art, and on male nudity in particular, reflected certain peculiarities in Greek culture. The role of the female was reduced to a minimum, and feelings of romantic love were displaced from relationships between men and women to those between mature men and youths. Ritual nudity was required at the athletic contests which played such an important role in the culture of the Greek city states, bringing otherwise hostile communities together in a

*'...No mightier spear than
that the champion hurls,
With which one night he fucked
three score of girls! '*

ANONYMOUS *19th century*

BELOW: **Erik Olson** *used the
male nude as a purely sexual
vehicle for expression. His
b-boy (sexual) fantasy series
6 has a pose derived from
Old Master paintings.*

spirit of regulated competition with strong religious overtones. To be naked in front of others was appropriate both to the victorious athlete and also to the being for whom he was a surrogate, the legendary hero.

The progression of Greek sculpture was essentially, until the fourth century BC, a progression through greater and greater mastery of the representation of the male. The whole system of proportions devised by Greek artists was based on the relationship of the various parts of the human body, and specifically that body in its masculine aspect.

Roman art took over the conventions of Greek art and added a few of its own. One of these was the marriage of realistic portraiture to the heroic nudity of the classical hero. There are a number of surviving cult statues of Roman emperors in which this forced conjunction produces a disturbing effect.

Christianity, with its central myth of Original Sin, personified by Adam and Eve and humanity's discovery of sexual shame after an act of disobedience to God's command, was naturally hostile to all representations of the unclothed body. Indeed, if the Ten Commandments were to be taken absolutely literally, one forbade any figurative representation whatsoever. The pagan tradition was, however, too deeply implanted, especially in Italy, to be permanently suppressed. As early as the mid-thirteenth

ABOVE: **George Dureau,,**
the New Orleans-based
artist began taking
photographs as studies
for his paintings. Dureau's
studies of Afro-American
models undoubtedly
influenced those of Robert
Mapplethorpe, who owned
several of his works. The
subject of this photograph
is Glenn Thompson.

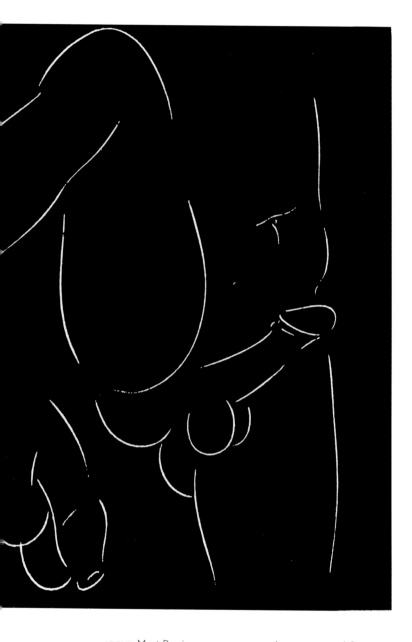

ABOVE: Most Precious
Ornament of 1937 by **Eric**
**Gill** (1882–1940) reveals his
fascination with his own
genitals. His habitual dress
code of long robe but no
underwear caused frequent
controversy, particularly
when he was working in
situ on sculpture from
scaffolding. Passers-by were
diverted, or outraged.

century we find the Italian sculptor Nicola Pisano
(fl. 1258–1278) reverting to classical prototypes. One of
his most important works, the pulpit in the Baptistery at
Pisa (1260), features a male nude – an allegory of
Strength – derived from the representations of Hercules
that are found on Roman sarcophagi.

As the revival of interest in classical antiquity gathered
strength in the fifteenth century, artists naturally turned
with passionate interest to rediscovered Roman
prototypes. The nude Adam in Masaccio's Brancacci
Chapel in Florence, which dates from c. 1427, has a
convincing solidity and realism which would have been
impossible without a knowledge of antique precedents.
The Eve who accompanies him is somewhat less
anatomically convincing.

There were reasons for this disparity which were
rooted in Renaissance workshop practice. Artists were
now emerging as independent creative personalities –
something much more than the mere artisans they had
been in the Middle Ages. Vasari's collection of *Lives*, a
series of biographies of well-known artists, was to codify
this when it was published in 1550, but the change itself
had begun more than a hundred years earlier. Remnants
of medieval practice remained, however, in particular the
custom whereby artists were organized in workshops,
headed by a master who might have journeyman
assistants, and who also trained a number of apprentices.
These workshops were entirely masculine affairs, and
when models were needed the artists posed for each
other. Drawings by Raphael (1485–1520) for some of his
Madonnas, for example, show that the first sketches were
made from young boys, in this case often fully clothed.

It became accepted that study of the male nude was
the essential route to becoming a fully professional artist.
Given the social conventions of the age, the idea that
artists might make studies of nude women was still an
unthinkable concept.

The situation was reinforced by other factors. One
was that Italian Renaissance art sprang from a
homoerotic culture. Not all leading artists were

## The Wingless & The Winged

'*the wingless*
*thing man . . .*
– e. e. cummings

*Most men use their cocks*
*for two things only:*
*they stand up pissing*
*& lie down fucking.*
*The world is full of horizontal men –*
*or vertical ones –*
*& really it is all the same disease.*

*But your cock flies*
*over the earth,*
*making shadows*
*on the bodies of women,*
*making wild bird noises*
*from its tiny mouth,*
*making music*
*& food for thought.*
*It is not a wingless thing*
*at all.*

*We could call it Pegasus –*
*if it didn't make us think*
*of gas stations.*
*Or we could call it Icarus –*
*if it didn't make us think*
*of falling.*

*But still it dips & dives*
*through the sky like a glider,*
*in search of a meadow,*
*a field,*
*a sun-dappled swamp*
*from which (you rightly said)*
*all life begins.*'

ERICA JONG *born 1942*

LEFT: **Tony Butcher's** *1990 photograph from his* Studies in Black *series is reminiscent of Magritte's paintings of women with their heads covered in drapery.*

'*The world is full of horizontal men − or vertical
ones − & really it is all the same disease.*'

ERICA JONG *born 1942*

THE WINGLESS & THE WINGED

homosexual, but a good number either preferred their own sex or were bisexual – among the names which come to mind are those of Donatello, Leonardo, Michelangelo, and Benvenuto Cellini. Michelangelo's example was especially influential. In the heroic David (1501–04) he allegorized the virtues of the threatened republican regime in Florence, and at the same time seemed to surpass the achievements of antiquity. His ceiling paintings in the Sistine Chapel (1508–12) show male nudes in the narrative scenes, notably in the memorable image of God creating Adam, but also use them in a purely arbitrary way, for decorative effect. The series of Ignudi which form part of the decorative framework of the ceiling were, for both contemporary and later artists, the most directly influential feature of the whole scheme.

At the end of the sixteenth century Michelangelo's work in the Sistine became the model for another ambitious decorative scheme – the ceiling painted by Annibale Carracci (1560–1609) with assistance from his brother Agostino (1557–1602) for the Palazzo Farnese in Rome. This scheme, too, features a series of heroic male nudes whose function is decorative not narrative. The Carracci brothers, with their cousin Lodovico (1556–1619) and various Bolognese followers, were responsible for codifying the teaching of art which now began to move away from the old workshop system towards a more formal, methodical and intellectual method of training. In this, too, study from the male nude, was essential, and female models, if now not entirely unknown, remained scarce.

Outside Italy, a number of major painters, particularly Rubens (1577–1640), showed a relish for depicting the female nude that presages a change of sensibility which

was not to show itself fully until the beginning of the eighteenth century. Though actual methods of training did not alter very much, the leading artists of the French Rococo, and in this case especially François Boucher, show a sharp reaction against the dominance of the male image. Boucher attracted the patronage of Louis XV's cultivated mistress Mme de Pompadour, and in response to this became the channel through which a

LEFT: **Bruce of Los Angeles** produced this twist on a 'classical' nude with an Elvis-style quiff; the model is Johnny Skaggs.

RIGHT: In **Bachardy's** Gilbert Haacke, 26 July 1977 the hair dates the image, while the T-shirt increases its erotic charge.

ABOVE: *In this drawing by* **Keith Vaughan** *(1912–77), the cropping of the picture preserves the individual* *anonymity of the model and accentuates the erotic curve and contours of the languidly sprawling limbs.*

new, feminized sensibility began to express itself. Many of his paintings feature female nudes disporting themselves in various ways – sometimes the settings are mythological, but sometimes they are purely domestic. In the mythological scenes in particular his female nudes often have equally nude male companions, and it is interesting to see what Boucher does with these. His preparatory drawings show that he was a powerful draughtsman, and that the male nude had no terrors for him. When these preparatory studies are transferred to paintings, however, the forms are routinely softened – Boucher's males become almost as deliciously soft and

chubby as his females. A similar process can be seen at work in the paintings of Jean-Honoré Fragonard (1732–1806).

The rise of Neo-Classicism, initiated by the stern German scholar Johann Joachim Winckelmann (1717–68), brought a reaction against this feminized sensibility. Winckelmann was homosexual, and he was motivated not only by scholarly urges but by a powerful subjective attachment to his own vision of Greek civilization, which for him provided an intellectual, physical and moral ideal which could be discovered nowhere else. Winckelmann's philosophy was enthusiastically taken up in France by a new generation of artists, in particular by Jacques-Louis David who imbibed Neo-Classical doctrines in Rome, and then initiated a revolution in French art with his powerful *Oath of the Horatii*, exhibited in the Salon of 1785.

' *Twenty-eight young men bathe by the shore,*
*Twenty-eight young men, and all so friendly,*
*Twenty-eight years of womanly life, and all so lonesome.*

*She owns the fine house by the rise of the bank,*
*She hides handsome and richly drest aft the blinds of the window.*

*Which of the young men does she like the best?*
*Ah the homeliest of them is beautiful to her.*

*Where are you off to, lady? for I see you,*
*You splash in the water there, yet stay stock still in your room.*

*Dancing and laughing along the beach came the twenty-ninth bather,*
*The rest did not see her, but she saw them and loved them.*

*The beards of the young men glistened with wet, it ran from their long hair,*
*Little streams passed all over their bodies.*

*An unseen hand also passed over their bodies,*
*It descended tremblingly from their temples and ribs.*

*The young men float on their backs, their white bellies swell to the sun . . . .*
*they do not ask who seizes fast to them,*
*They do not know who puffs and declines with pendant and bending arch,*
*They do not think whom they souse with spray.* '

WALT WHITMAN *1819–92*
LEAVES OF GRASS 1855

BELOW: *The mosaic of Jael*
*and Sisera (c.1680) was*
*commissioned for St Peter's in*
*Rome from* **Carlo Maratta**
*(1625–1713). This study*
*for the figure of Sisera was*
*not intended to be erotic –*
*any erotic content*
*is the result of a*
*modern interpretation.*

'*O the difference of man and man… I was amazed
and enlightened by the variety of the male organ. In the
rank and file of men showering the cocks and balls took on
the air almost of an independent species, exhibited in
instructive contrasts. Here was the long, listless penis,
there the curt athletic knob or innocent rosebud
of someone scarcely out of school.*'

ALAN HOLLINGHURST
THE SWIMMING POOL LIBRARY 1988

BELOW: **Don Bachardy,**
*companion of the writer
Christopher Isherwood,
specializes in portrait-like
studies of the male nude, such
as* Robert Ward, 9 Sept 1986.

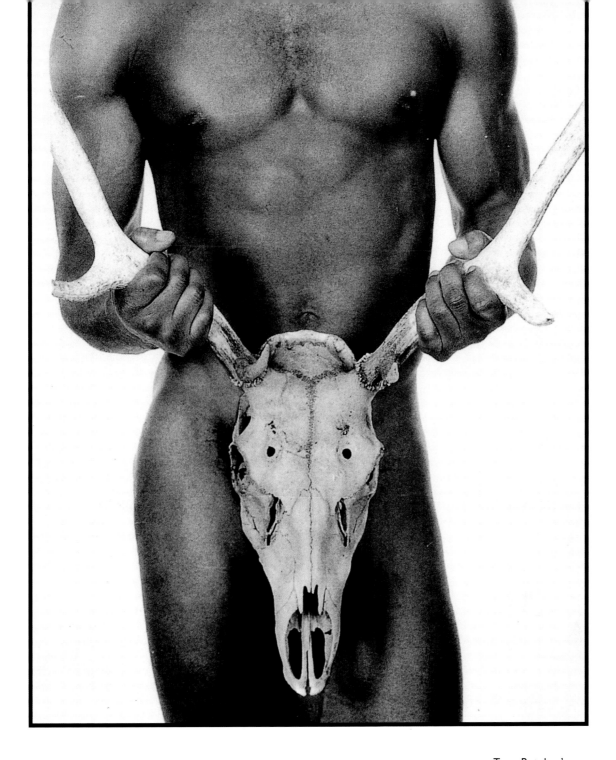

ABOVE: **Tony Butcher's** *1996 fine torso study from his* Studies in Black *series of photographs is a different twist on a familiar theme from the work of Georgia O'Keeffe.*

ABOVE: **Bachardy's** Danny
Wade Dalton, 12 October
1977 *is another example
of his spontaneous,
immediate portrait nudes
produced, as the titles
suggest, after a single
sitting by the model.*

Though it was in fact a royal commission, the *Oath of
the Horatii* was interpreted as a trumpet blast against the
already crumbling French monarchy, and David went on
to identify himself with the political convulsion initiated
in 1789. He became a member of the Convention, voted
for the death of Louis XVI, and barely escaped with his
life when his ally Robespierre fell in 1794. In addition to
leading a tumultuous political existence, David also
initiated a reform in the system of teaching art, and his
influence in this sphere was greatly increased by his
identification with the Napoleonic regime. His subject
pictures of this period, especially his long-meditated
*Leonidas*, which Napoleon visited David's studio to see
during the Hundred Days, demonstrated his own interest
in the heroic male nude.

The system of training he initiated, essentially a
rethinking of that already set up by the Carracci, was to
remain in force throughout the nineteenth century, and
extended its influence to most European countries and to
the United States as well. It could not, however, wholly
resist the changes which were taking place in the
audience for art. A new bourgeois public showed an
eager appetite for subject-matter which appealed to
hedonistic rather than learned tastes. Its preference was
for female nudes rather than male ones, and academically
trained painters hastened to supply the market as soon as
their education was finished and they were able to set up
independent careers. One thing which helped them in
this endeavour was that the long-standing prejudice
against female models had now entirely broken down.
'Respectable' women, aristocratic or bourgeois, did not
pose nude, except in wholly exceptional circumstances.
Nevertheless painters found a ready supply of models –
and often mistresses as well – among the members of the
new urban working class.

Academic paintings of the female nude – the kind of
thing which appeared in the annual Salons in Paris and in
the Summer Exhibitions held by the Royal Academy in
London – generally still favoured mythological or
allegorical themes or, failing this, found some exotic

'*A fair slim boy, not made for*
*this world's pain,*
*With hair of gold, thick-clustering*
*around his ears,*
*And longing eyes, half veiled*
*by foolish tears*
*Like bluest water seen*
*through mists of rain:*
*Pale cheeks whereon no love*
*hath left its stain.*'

OSCAR WILDE 1854–1900
LILY GIRL 1881

BELOW: **Bachardy's** *more recent work has a more Expressionist mood. Tom Long, 20 August 1996 is reminiscent of Egon Schiele's work.*

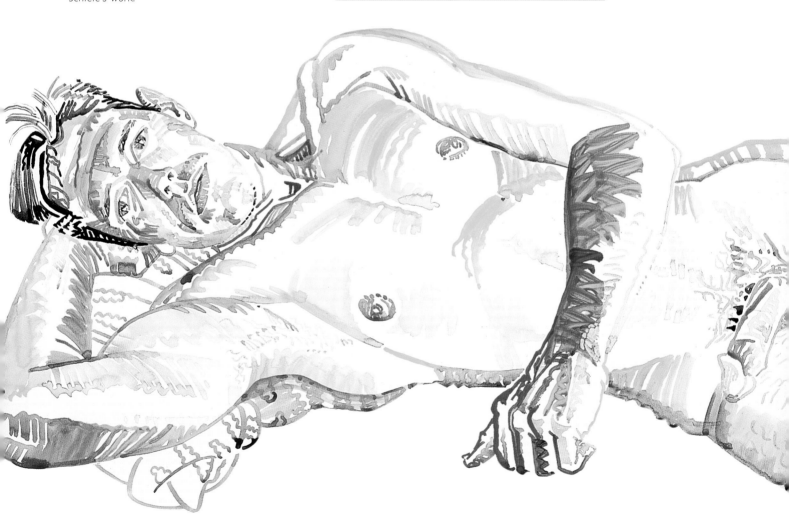

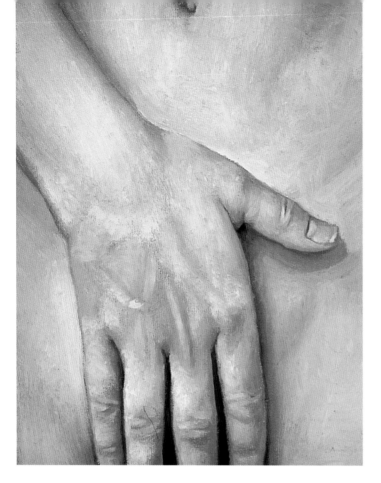

## Undressing

' *Stripping off, peeling, shucking*
*– getting ready to offer*
*(with so many half-mutttered*
*shame-faced excuses) yourself.*
*How could I refuse you now?*
*The heat in the room is not*
*merely the fire or the drink.*
*It rises up from my heart.*
*I love you for making this gift,*
*though now it is mine I am*
*no longer perfectly sure*
*that I truthfully want it.*
*And yet how touchng they are,*
*those small unknown details*
*which enter the stage one by*
*one. A mole. A gold chain. A*
*nipple. A scar. I number*
*them gratefully now, the small*
*tokens – now it is over.* '

EDWARD LUCIE-SMITH

pretext for nudity. Orientalist harem scenes, a genre initiated by David's artistic heir Jean-Auguste-Dominique Ingres (1780–1867) were especially popular. This could not disguise the fact that the whole educational framework which had sustained the painting of the past, and which had given it many of its major themes (the others being derived from Christian doctrine), was now in terminal decline.

The rise of Modernism, which destroyed the old academic system without putting anything in its place, meant that artists had to struggle to give new meaning to depictions of both the male and the female nude. Both tended to be reduced to one very simple message: they became emblems of eroticism, pure and simple, without the additional messages which had been attached to such representations in the past. On the whole both artists and public found it easier to deal with the female nude in these circumstances, and the male nude dropped almost entirely from view. Its recent revival, particularly in photography, is closely linked to increased tolerance of male homosexuality and to the strength of the 'rainbow coalition' of minority interests which forms the post-modernist consensus.

ABOVE LEFT: *Young Scottish artist* **Alison Watt** *has cunningly cropped this composition, entitled* Body # 4 *of 1996, thus emphasizing the inherent eroticism through the concealing gesture.*

'*...the heat in the room is not merely the fire or the drink...*'

EDWARD LUCIE-SMITH
UNDRESSING

ABOVE: *This is an unusual painting by leading Bolognese Academician* **Giovanni Lanfranco** *(1582–1647) The homosexuality of the model is implied by the cat and coquettish glances over the sitter's shoulder.*

RIGHT: Bacchante with a
Bunch of Grapes *by*
**Jacques Antoine Vallin**
*(1760–1831), a minor
French painter of the*

*Neo-Classical epoch. His
robust nude owes much to
Rubens in her form, and
the coyly held grapes stress
the theme of abundance.*

# Naked as EVE

*t*he female nude in art has a much more problematic history than representations of the male. Or this had been the case until quite recently. Some of the earliest known works of art are representations of nude females, and the impulse to make these can be assumed to be deeply rooted in the human psyche. The very oldest are the statuettes showing steatopygous women found at certain Palaeolithic sites. The most famous example is the Venus from Willendorf in Austria, generally dated to between 30,000 and 25,000 BC.

The Willendorf sculpture exaggerates all the characteristics which are signifiers of fertility. She has plump buttocks, a large, perhaps pregnant, belly, and vast nurturing breasts. What she lacks is facial features – any human individuality.

The civilizations of the Ancient Near East made representations of nude females. The conventions followed are more or less those seen in the Venus of Willendorf, with a lesser degree of exaggeration. In some ways they are more 'abstract' than their Palaeolithic exemplar, in the sense that rather than the body being seen as a whole these figures are conceptual accretions of sexual parts. This tendency is taken to an extreme in a multi-breasted cult statuette sometimes called the 'Diana of the Ephesians'. Here the normally chaste goddess becomes an aspect of Cybele, the Great Mother.

'*What's the matter, why do you groan and grunt?*
*Is all this fuss because you want my cunt?*
*Take it, go on then, you can have it all*
*Saints preserve us! damn! but you love it well!*
*If I could put a price on my belle chose*
*And sell it, I'd walk as fresh as a rose.*
*But I will keep it for your own sweet tooth;*
*By God, you are to blame to tell the truth.*'

GEOFFREY CHAUCER 1340–1400
THE WIFE OF BATH'S PROLOGUE

The Ancient Egyptians, from whom Greek art inherited so much, seldom made representations of female nudes. Such as they did make usually form part of trivial domestic objects, such as an elegant toilet spoon, where the handle is formed as a swimming girl. There are also stylized female figures, usually described as dolls. More significant than these, for my present purpose, are Egyptian representations of women in extremely close fitting, transparent, often pleated dresses. These reveal sexual characteristics almost as clearly as if the subjects had been naked. One of the finest of these representations is the small torso of an Amarna princess now in the Louvre. Interestingly, this carries over important characteristics from Palaeolithic sculpture. Though the breasts of the figure are small, to the point of being underdeveloped, her belly and buttocks have been deliberately exaggerated.

In Archaic Greek art, the convention was for statues of *korai*, or maidens, to be elaborately clothed, while their male equivalents, the *kouroi*, are shown naked. Nude women do, however, make frequent appearances in vase-paintings. Often the scenes in which they appear make it clear that they are *hetaeras*, or professional courtesans. Despite this, the usual female type seen in vase-paintings tends to be boyish rather than voluptuous – the women have sinewy legs, flat stomachs and small, firm, high breasts. When shown

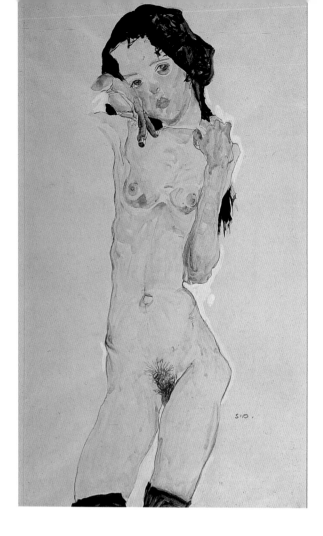

ABOVE: **Egon Schiele's**
*superbly drafted* Nude
*(1910) evokes the*
*awkward adolescent form.*

' Like a fisherwoman at an angling hole,
patiently waiting for a bite, she moved about
on her heels, the tip of my penis between
her labia. At last, when the rake of both penis
and pubis had matched to her satisfaction,
she settled down and let my penis enter her
vagina. She bobbed away energetically,
glancing briefly at herself in the dressing-
table mirror, and now and then blowing the
hair from her eyes. '

J . G . BALLARD *born 1930*
THE KINDNESS OF WOMEN 1991

with males, even in sexually explicit situations, their
gestures tend to be comradely rather than seductive. In
one vase-painting, for example, a nude girl
compassionately holds up the head of a drunken young
boy who is vomiting.

In the fourth century BC the situation changed, and
there was a sudden upsurge of interest in the female nude
as a subject for life-size sculpture. Basically there are two
types, each associated with a celebrated sculptor of the
time. One was Scopas, the chief artist of the Mausoleum
of Halicarnassus. His vision of the nude was the athletic
one we see on Greek vases. The nude and semi-nude
female figures associated with his school are usually
characterized either as Amazons – female warriors – or as
maenads – the ecstatic female followers of Dionysus.

Much more influential was a second type, whose
creation is attributed to the sculptor Praxiteles. In
antiquity, Praxiteles' most famous creation was the
Aphrodite of Cnidus, a nude figure of the goddess of love
emerging from her bath. The woman is totally naked,
with a soft, voluptuous, slightly thick-waisted figure. The
spectator is asked to imagine that she has been surprised
at her ablutions. She holds a towel in one hand and
shields her sex with the other.

The Aphrodite of Cnidus spawned further variants of
the same theme in Hellenistic times. Women, in the guise
of goddesses, were shown both nude and partly nude. In
one particularly influential composition, Aphrodite
clutches a towel to her breasts, which falls to cover most
of the front of her torso. At the same time she thrusts
back her exposed buttocks, which thus become the chief
focus of sexual attention. The Aphrodite Kallipygos'
'beautiful bottom', as this type was called, enjoyed a long
period of popularity and was revived in the Renaissance.

Though her gesture of modesty is somewhat half-
hearted, the Aphrodite of Cnidus already embodies the idea
of the female as the victim of the male gaze. This idea was
strongly emphasized in Christian art. In the art of the early
and high Middle Ages, Aphrodite was replaced by Eve, the
embodiment of sexual shame. In the first part of the

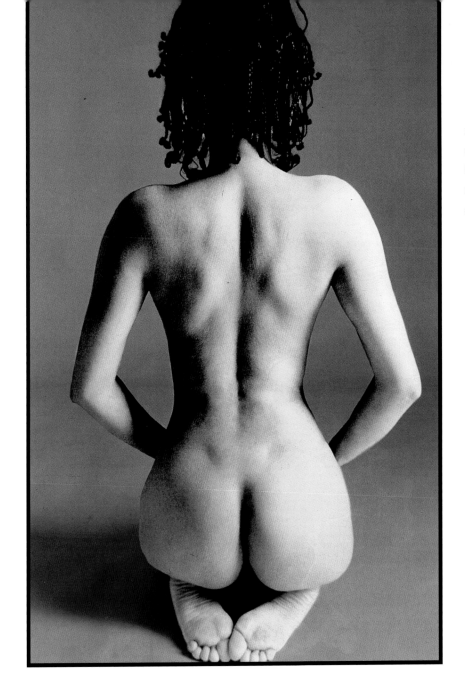

'*Her slender arms, her soft and supple back,*
*Her tapered sides — all fleshy, smooth and white —*
*He stroked, and asked for favours at her neck,*
*Her snowish throat, her breasts so round and light;*
*Thus in this heaven he took his delight,*
*And smothered her with kisses upon kisses,*
*Till gradually he came to learn where bliss is.*'

GEOFFREY CHAUCER *1340–1400*
TROILUS AND CRISEYDE

ABOVE: *The reclining nude has beckoned alluringly from her couch or chaise-longue to many artists over the centuries. This seductive, elegant photograph by*

**Frank Herbolt** *pays homage to Antonio Canova's celebrated, coolly erotic sculpture of Paulina Borghese (1805–07), the beautiful sister of the Emperor Napoleon.*

'Have you beheld (with much delight)
A red rose peeping through a white?
Or else a cherry (double graced)
Within a lilly? Centre placed?
Or ever marked the pretty beam,
A strawberry shows half drowned in cream?
Or seen rich rubies blushing through
A pure smooth pearl, and orient too?
So like to this, nay all the rest,
Is each neat niplet of her breast.'

ROBERT HERRICK 1591–1674
UPON THE NIPPLES OF JULIA'S BREAST

ABOVE: However draped in the respectable cloak of history, a nude is a nude is a nude. In the Tepidarium (1881) by **Sir Lawrence Alma-Tadema** (1836–1912) the bather reclining in a meticulously researched classical setting, is really no more than an excuse to show a handsome nude, her genitalia coyly covered by a strategic ostrich feather.

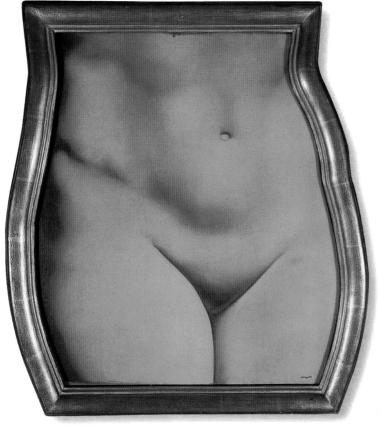

'My thighs were exquisitely fashioned but what infinitely enriched and adorned them was the sweet intersection formed where they met at the bottom of the smoothest, roundest white belly.'

JOHN CLELAND *1709–89*
FANNY HILL 1749

ABOVE: *By enclosing a female torso in a frame fitting its contours,* **René Magritte** *(1898–1967) questions the relationship between reality and the painted image in his* La Representation *of 1937.*

period at least, art again passed from a perceptual into a purely conceptual mode. The nude female body, in its rare appearances, was imagined not directly observed. This meant that female figures tended to be made up of standard parts, just as they had been in the art of the Ancient Near East.

If the story of the Fall offered the commonest occasion for representing nude women, there were other biblical pretexts. One was the story of Susanna, another that of Bathsheba.

One noticeable thing about female nudes of the late medieval period is the way in which the female body is made to conform to the current fashion in dress. The nudes of this time are long-legged, high-waisted, small-breasted, with slightly protuberant, pregnant-looking bellies. This exactly matches the fashionable ideal of the time, as expressed through clothing.

Nudes of this type also populate early Renaissance secular representations of naked females. One of the first artists to make such paintings was the German, Lucas Cranach the Elder (1472–1553), court painter to the Electors of Saxony, who were prominent supporters of the Reformation and leaders of the Protestant cause against the papacy. Their taste for paintings of the nude, and especially the female nude, may in this context seem like a paradox, since Protestant theology took an even more vehemently hostile view of sexual sins than the version of Christianity it was trying to replace. The explanation is at least partly political. The Protestant rulers in early sixteenth-century Germany were also the pioneers of a new secularism. They wanted to create a situation where the ruler exercised control over the religious authorities in his territory. Hedonistic representations of the female nude were a covert assertion of the supremacy of the secular arm.

A somewhat similar spirit was present in France, though the kings of France maintained their allegiance to the Catholic Church. The conspicuously pagan decorations of the great palace at Fontainebleau were an expression of independence from papal decrees. They are a defiant assertion of royal and aristocratic privilege. It was the king's right, and that of the great men who surrounded him, to look at things which were forbidden to those who occupied a lower place in the social scale.

Cranach's nudes and those painted for Fontainebleau by both French and Italian artists adhere, not to the classical canon of proportions then being reintroduced in Italy, the fountainhead of artistic innovation, but to the physical type already described which was inherited from the late Middle Ages.

The seventeenth and eighteenth centuries witnessed a gradual loosening of restraints, to the point where the female nude became one of the central subjects of European art. Body types changed in conformity to fashion. The heavy, voluptuous nudes of Rubens are altogether different from the slender beauties favoured by Mannerist artists at Fontainebleau.

At the beginning of the eighteenth century, in particular, there was an upsurge in erotic representations of all kinds, and especially the representation of the nude female. In French Rococo painting both the accoutrements used and the poses direct the spectator's attention to specific erogenous zones in a much more insistent way than had been the case previously. The favoured area is not the genitalia, still considered a forbidden aspect, to be discreetly glimpsed perhaps but not boldly examined, nor even the breasts, but the buttocks. The epoch's fixation on this part of the body is attested to by the erotic texts of the time, as well as by what appears in art. De Sade's unfortunate heroine Justine, for example, is repeatedly chastized and also repeatedly buggered by her master.

A fetishistic obsession with the female buttocks was to have a long career in Western art and literature. It features powerfully in the drawings and prints of the Surrealist artist Hans Bellmer (1902–75), and is a theme in two famous erotic books – D.H. Lawrence's *Lady Chatterley's Lover* and 'Pauline Réage's' *The Story of O*. When the gamekeeper Mellors, Lawrence's embodiment of the natural man, takes Connie Chatterley anally, this symbolizes both the final breakdown of her inhibitions and his complete possession of her.

ABOVE: *An unusually sensual and informal image for its time by* **Giovanni Guercino** *(1591–1666),* Woman Undressing, *c. 1620, seems to have been drawn from life, in spite of the Church's vehement disapproval of the presence of females in any artist's studio.*

' *Away with silk,*
*away with lawn,*
*I'll have no scenes*
*curtains drawn…*

ROBERT HERRICK
*1591–1674*
CLOTHES DO BUT CHEAT
AND COZEN US

ABOVE: **Lorne Resnick's** *depiction*
*of a female torso swathed in silk*
*clearly shows the influence of*
*Hellenistic Greek sculptors, who*
*frequently wrapped their goddesses*
*and nymphs in diaphanous fabrics.*

In *The Story of O*, the victim-heroine is always used anally by her aristocratic English lover.

Erotic emphases have nevertheless shifted once again since the eighteenth century. In twentieth-century pin-ups, the emphasis tends to be more on the breasts than on the buttocks. The ideal pin-up resembles an Indian *apsara* or divine maiden, sinuous, with voluptuous hips and breasts divided by a wasp waist.

One of the things which has greatly changed attitudes to the female nude has been the advent of photography. As I have noted in the introduction to this book, the camera is seen as sometimes peculiarly aggressive and intrusive. It is also seen as a way of taking possession of something, a person or an object, and perhaps also as an instrument which can be used to reduce human beings to the status of objects. Yet the camera also has powers to remake what it sees, and in addition to this it demonstrates how human beings go to great trouble to remake themselves physically, so as to conform to the notion of desirability prevalent during a particular era. Thus, where erotic photographs taken in the mid-nineteenth century show plump, almost fat, little women with well-developed busts, those which were taken in the 1920s – the era of the flapper – offer girls who are slim, lithe and boyish.

A question which arises here is that of what, if any, answers can be made to the feminist condemnation of images of nude women. One reply is certainly to be found in the sheer length of time during which they have been made. It would be difficult to find anything more integral to human culture. Obviously the male impulse to produce such things is very deeply rooted in the human psyche.

RIGHT: *Another silk-wrapped goddess pays homage to the Hellenistic style in a photograph by* **David Hanover.**

Another point is to note the extent to which this condemnation seems to be based on class, perhaps just as much as it is on gender. Essentially images of the female nude now tend to be identified with blue-collar rather than white-collar tastes. They are, as the Pop movement divined, one of the indicators of mass culture. Those who make such images may be highly remunerated. So, too, very often are those who pose for them, who strip for the camera of their own free choice. The spectators, however, are assumed to belong to the brutish mass. The attitudes encouraged by the photographs are then, so the argument runs, projected on to all women.

The distaste felt for the pin-up, and, because of the pin-up, for all representations of the female nude is undoubtedly visceral, and its strength should not be underestimated. The problem arises in the context of a free society: by attempting to ban a particular kind of activity, and, in particular, by attempting to ban a particular sort of image, we not only tend to create conditions in which injustices are likely to occur but we are also demanding the impossible. Where the Church failed, modern feminism is unlikely to succeed. The new digital technologies make the possibility of a successful ban several degrees more unlikely.

## The Long Tunnel of Wanting You

' *This is the long tunnel of wanting you.*
*Its walls are lined with remembered kisses*
*wet & red as the inside of your mouth,*
*full & juicy as your probing tongue,*
*warm as your belly against mine,*
*deep as your navel leading home,*
*soft as your sleeping cock beginning to stir,*
*tight as your legs wrapped around mine,*
*straight as your toes pointing toward the bed*
*as you roll over & thrust your hardness*
*into the long tunnel of my wanting,*
*seeding it with dreams & unbearable hope,*
*making memories of the future,*
*straightening out my crooked past,*
*teaching me to live in the present present tense*
*with the past perfect and the uncertain future*
*suddenly certain for certain*
*in the long tunnel of my old wanting*
*which before always had an ending*
*but now begins & begins again*
*with you, with you, with you.* '

ERICA JONG *born 1942*

LEFT: *The very basic nature of sexuality is stressed in* You Like Pork?, *the 1995 painting by Chinese artist* **Liu Wei**. *A central nude is surrounded by a frame of multiple images of cuts of meat.*

ABOVE: *In* I Hear *of 1988,* **Francesco Clemente** *has created a potent sexual emblem by replacing a woman's head by a flower, a visual metaphor for the vulva.*

'*Ah God, ah God,*
*that night when we two clung*
*So close, our hungry lips*
*Transfused into each our*
*hovering souls,*
*Mortality's eclipse!*'

PETRONIUS ARBITER
TRS. HELEN WADDELL

BELOW: *This striking*
*photograph of* Woman's
Lips *by* **Bruce Ayres** *uses*
*a strongly erotic body part*
*to represent the whole.*

cropping focuses the
spectator's attention on the
sexual possibilities offered by
the naked woman lying on
the bed.

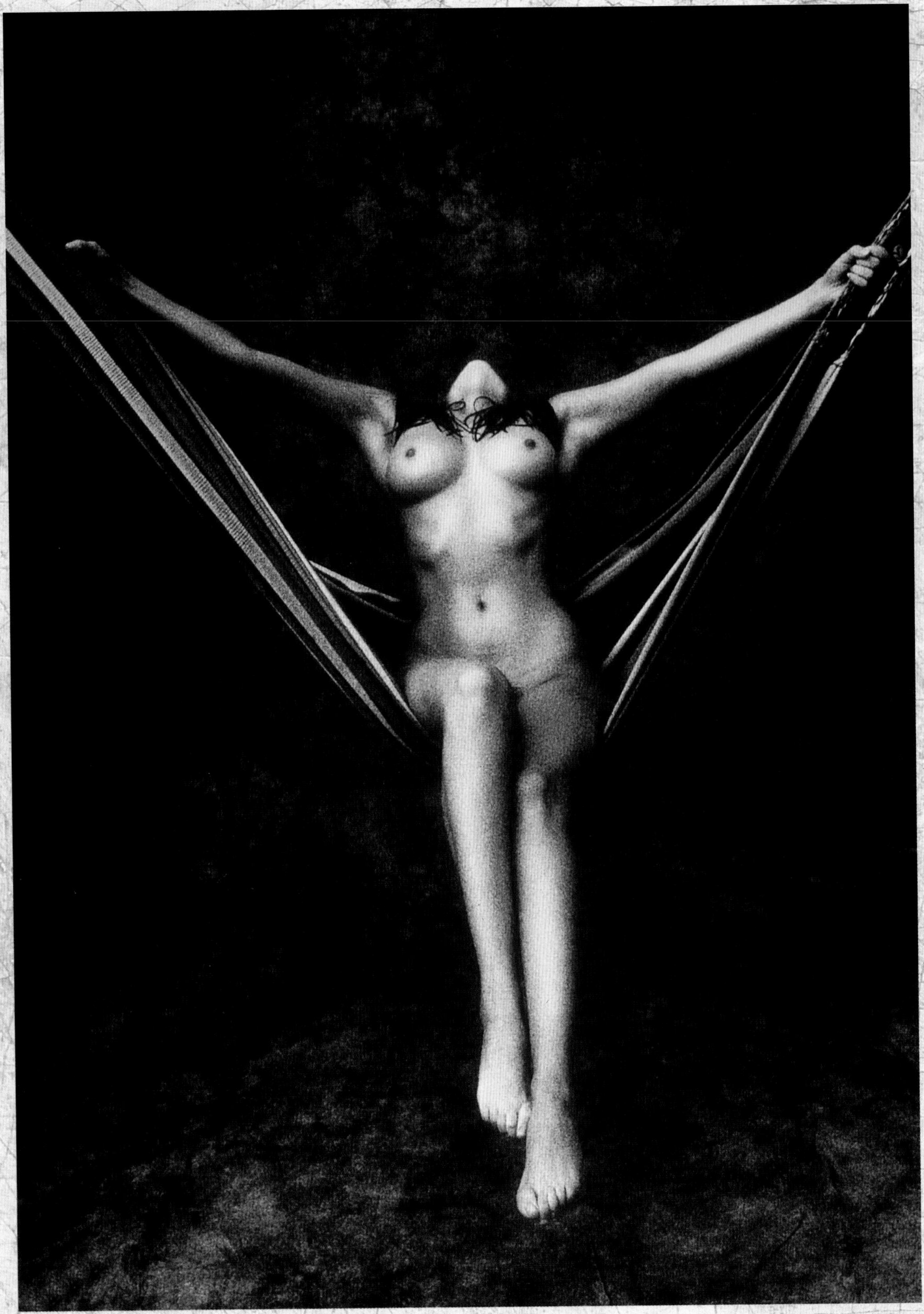

LEFT: **Stefan May** *uses a hammock to suspend the figure of his nude, her throat stretched taut in ecstasy, giving the impression of orgasmic flight.*

' *Full nakedness! All joye are due to thee,*
*As souls unbodied, bodies uncloth'd must be,*
*To taste whole joys. Gems which you women use*
*Are like Atlanta's balls, cast in men's views,*
*That when a fools eye lighteth on a Gem,*
*His earthly soul may covet theirs, not them.*
*Like pictures, or like books gay coverings made*
*For lay-men, are all women thus array'd;*
*Themselves are mystick books, which only wee*
*(Whom are imputed grace will dignifie)*
*Must see reveal'd. Then since that I may know;*
*As liberally, as to a Midwife, shew*
*Thy self: cast all, yea, this white lynnen hence,*
*Here is no penance, much less innocence.*
*To teach thee, I am naked first; why then*
*What needst thou have more covering then a man.* '

J O H N   D O N N E   *1572–1631*
GOING TO BED
(ELEGY XIX)

ABOVE: *In his picture of a woman emerging from clouds in a pool,* **Andrew Rodney** *has cleverly used several negatives to produce an effect reminiscent of Baroque altarpieces.*

*51*

LEFT: **Pierre Bonnard** *(1867–1947) painted many pictures of his wife Marthe. In 1899, before their marriage, Bonnard depicted her as a reclining nude in this intimate study.*

ABOVE: *Blurred image and clever use of configuration express the scale of the woman's ecstasy as she abandons herself to pleasure. This picture is by* **Jean François Gaté.**

'*Your love has gone all through my body*
*Like honey in water,*
*As a drug is mixed into spices*
*As water is mingled with wine...*'

EGYPTIAN LOVE LYRIC

ABOVE: Rolla *painted by*
**Henri Gervex** *(1852–1929)*
*in 1878 caused major*
*scandal when first exhibited.*
*It depicts a suicidal young*
*man in the aftermath*
*of a passionate night*
*with a courtesan.*

' *Young homosexuals and girls in love,*
*and widows gone to seed, sleepless, delirious,*
*and novice housewives pregnant some thirty hours,*
*the hoarse cats cruising across my garden's shadows*
*like a necklace of throbbing, sexual oysters*
*surround my solitary home*
*like enemies entrenched against my soul,*
*like conspirators in pyjamas*
*exchanging long, thick kisses on the sly.* '

PABLO NERUDA *1904–73*
TRS. NATHANIEL TARN
LONE GENTLEMAN

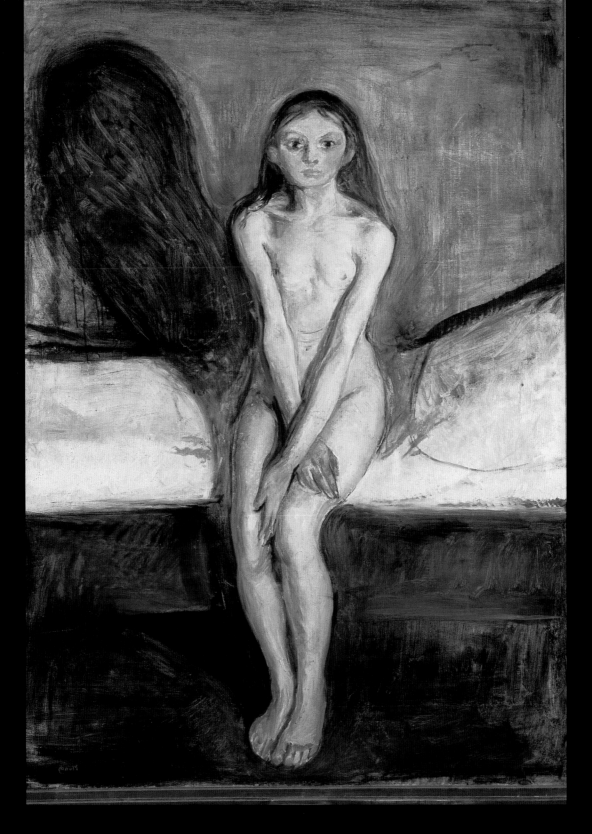

ABOVE: *Early in his prolific career* **Edvard Munch** *(1863–1944) painted* Puberty, *his famous image about sexual awakening. The girl is startled by her unfamiliar feelings and emotions.*

# Loves of the
# GODS

**f**rom the Renaissance until the end of the eighteenth century – and perhaps even a little beyond – European images of erotic subjects made use, more often than not, of the framework of classical mythology. Since this framework is now unfamiliar to most of us, it is useful to know how the mechanism worked, and what advantages it offered to students of erotica.

For educated people, during this half-millennium, the pagan world, and the texts connected with it, offered a kind of parallel universe to the everyday one which was, of course, throughout this period dominated by Christianity. The whole system of education was in fact largely founded on Greek and Latin texts. While there was an inclination to interpret these in a Christian sense wherever possible, sometimes forcing the intended meaning quite severely in order to do so (the study of Plato was a case in point), the pagan writers said things, and tackled subjects, which were otherwise considered to be forbidden territory.

Knowledge of these texts was one of the things which separated the learned and sophisticated, therefore usually well-born and prosperous man, from the vulgar mass. It is not surprising, therefore, that people of this kind, generically those who had the means to commission artists, liked paintings and other works of art with pagan subject-matter. Immediate recognition of slightly recondite themes formed a bond between members of the privileged group – it was one of the ways in which they marked the difference between themselves and the rest of the world.

*' It is a kind of pleasing thing,*
*A pricking and a piercing sting.*
*It is Venus' wanton wand.*
*It hath no legs and yet can stand.*
*A bachelor's button thoroughly ripe,*
*The kindest new tobacco pipe.*
*It is the pen that Helen took*
*To write in her two-leaved book.*
*It's a prick-shaft of Cupid's cut,*
*Yet some do shoot it at a butt.*
*And every wench by her good will*
*Would keep it in her quiver still.*
*The fairest yet that e'er had life*
*For love of this became a wife.'*

ANONYMOUS
*17th century*

Until the rise of the new mercantile bourgeois society in Holland at the beginning of the seventeenth century, themes taken from pagan mythology formed the staple of secular as opposed to religious painting. Dutch patrons were the first to find more interest in art which directly reflected the world around them, rather than attempting to conjure up the lost universe of antiquity. And even Dutch painters, particularly those who had worked for a while in Italy, tackled these themes from time to time.

All Renaissance and post-Renaissance painting was founded, as we have already seen, on the study of the nude. Knowledge of the nude was certainly required in order to paint religious works. Crucifixion scenes, also those showing violent martyrdoms (St Sebastian, St Bartholomew, St Laurence), often featured naked or nearly naked protagonists. In this case, nudity was more or less concomitant with pain and violence. Decorative mythological scenes allowed for a contrast between male and female bodies usually not possible in religious art.

The firm division which patrons, even very devout ones, made in their minds between devotional paintings and those made for purely secular use can be seen in what Philip II of Spain, the most important artistic patron of his time, ordered from his favourite artist, Titian (c. 1480s–1576). Titian's female nudes are perhaps the most sensual of their epoch – an example is his *Venus and the Organ Player,* one of the paintings Philip II ordered from him. The artist always justified them, however, by giving them a mythological gloss. The difference in emotional tone can easily be gauged by putting another mythological nude by Titian, the *Venus of Urbino (1538),* beside Manet's *Olympia (1865),* which is derived directly from it. The nineteenth-century critics who denounced

BELOW: *This image of Mars and Venus (c. 1580–90), the most famous lovers in Greek mythology, was painted by a member of the accomplished School of* Prague who worked for the sixteenth-century Habsburg Emperor Rudolph II, known for his penchant for erotic scenes based on mythological situations.

the *Olympia* as indecent did so essentially because the artist seemed to stress the fact that what was shown was not a mythological being, but a contemporary woman who happened to have shed her clothes and who, worse still, was not at all worried by her own nudity.

If mythology served to excuse and even, in a certain sense, to sanctify depictions of the female nude, it became still more essential to the painter when he wanted to show several nude figures in conjunction with one another, especially if these figures were of an opposite sex. Luckily artists did not have to look far to find a justificatory source: the collection of legends concerning the loves of the pagan gods put together by the Latin poet Ovid. Though Virgil was more respected as a writer, and Horace perhaps better loved, Ovid was the most accessible of the Latin poets to a post-classical age. His retelling of classical legends appealed not only through the vividness of his descriptions, but through a certain lightness and irony of tone. He purveys eroticism, but at

ABOVE: *There is an exquisite eroticism about* **Jean-Antoine Watteau's** Nymph and Satyr, *enhanced by the satyr's gesture and the figures' contrasting flesh tones.*

the same time distances it, defuses it, removes any feeling of threat or danger. This was exactly the feeling the painters wanted to convey.

Ovid had already enjoyed great popularity in the Middle Ages, from the twelfth century onwards. Traces of his influence can be found in many medieval romances, including the most ambitious of them, the *Roman de la Rose*. But not until the Renaissance was it possible to illustrate his work in a wholly uninhibited way. Both *The Art of Love* (1 BC) and the *Metamorphoses* (AD 2) offered themes which were eagerly taken up. A frequently illustrated passage, for instance, comes from *The Art of Love*, which describes the smith-god Vulcan's revenge on his wife Venus, and her lover Mars, the god of war.

ABOVE: *This elaborate photographic composition is German and dates from c. 1900. It was obviously made by using a system of mirrors. The down-to earth realism with which the faces and the bodies of the models is shown contrasts amusingly with their use as atlantes (heroic figures based on the Titan Atlas, who in Greek mythology held up the world) supporting a classical cornice.*

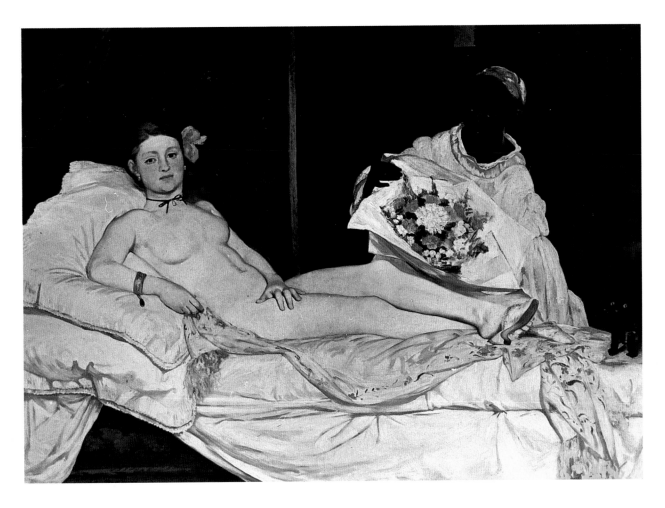

' So Vulcan set hidden
Snares around and over the bed (no eye
Could detect them), then put it about that he was off to Lemnos.
The lovers
Met as arranged, were trapped
In the toils, lay naked: tableau. Then Vulcan invited
All the gods round. Venus was close to tears –
She and Mars couldn't cover their faces, couldn't even
Move a hand to their private parts.
Someone laughed and said: "If you find your chains a burden,
Brave Mars, transfer them to me!"
At Neptune's urging, reluctantly, Vulcan released them:
Venus ran off to Paphos, Mars to Thrace.
So much for Vulcan's plotting: once their shameful
Secret was out, the lovers did as they pleased
Without thought for concealment. '

OVID, TRANS. PETER GREEN
THE ART OF LOVE

ABOVE: *In his infamous
1863 painting Olympia,*
**Edouard Manet** *used the
composition of Titian's
Venus of Urbino to affront
Parisian society with a
realistic woman, confident
despite her nudity.*

ABOVE: *An unidealized nude, typical of* **Rembrandt** *(1606–69), but drawn in the untypical medium of red chalk. The asp tells us that she is Cleopatra, 'with Phoebus' amorous pinches bruised black'.*

One of the ways in which artists distanced both themselves and their audience from the full erotic impact of scenes like this was through the use of ever more ingenious and elaborate settings and poses. These offered reassurance that such acts took place only in fantasy. At the same time the ingeniously contorted poses offered painters and sculptors an opportunity to show off their virtuoso skills in depicting the figure.

Artists had other methods of defence as well. The most important was one which they inherited directly from the Greek and Roman world – the use of transformation and metaphor. Erotic scenes are relatively commonplace, for example, on Greek vases. But it is noticeable that there is a certain gradation. The wilder and more erotic the scene, the more likely it is that the participants will be only half-human. That is, they will not be men and women but the goat-legged, cloven-hoofed satyrs who were the merrily rebellious followers of Dionysus, the god of altered states.

The fundamental basis of Greek mythology, and therefore of Roman mythology as well, was the search for metaphors which would describe and personify the forces of nature. For all their irony and frivolity, this is what the stories in Ovid's *Metamorphoses* are really about. The transformation into a laurel tree of a nymph fleeing from a god, the shed blood of Venus' mortal lover Adonis giving birth to anemones – these are oblique ways of saying that the natural world is fundamentally a unity, fecund and perpetually renewed.

One cannot say that the Renaissance and Baroque painters who made use of classical myth as a way of both expressing and excusing erotic content consciously knew this, but their very use of mythology linked them to themes which were very ancient. This, however, was of much less practical importance than the fact that by placing sexual gestures, even fairly forthright and candid ones, within a framework of classical myth, the artist was able both to have his cake and eat it. And this was true for the spectators as well. A whole palace, like sixteenth-century Fontainebleau, could be filled with sumptuous decorations bristling with nude figures, but there was no suggestion that their presence was a direct encouragement to sexual activity.

It is interesting to note that there always seems to have been a kind of hierarchy, not so much in what was shown, but in how it was shown – how it became available. One of the things which appeared almost simultaneously with the revival of the mythological apparatus in Western art was the invention of printing. A printed image is public in a different sense from a large

ABOVE: *In* Hercules and
Omphale *(c.1730) by*
**François Boucher**, *the less
muscular hero embraces the
woman who will force him to
wear women's clothing.*

'*She laid her fingers on
his manly cheek,*'

MICHAEL DRAYTON
1563–1631
THE BARON'S WARS, CANTO SIX

RIGHT: *When Christ rose from the dead, the only people to see Him were two women followers, Mary Magdalene and Mary the sister of Martha. In* **Scott Seidman's** *1992 picture, He has Risen II, this fact is taken into account.*

decorative painting or a life-sized sculpture. It goes from hand to hand. It is perhaps shared with friends. But its real function is to be contemplated in private. Art, in this form, ceases to be a collective experience and becomes a purely individual communication, offered by one sensibility, received by another. Once Romano's *I Modi* were circulated, accompanied by Pietro Aretino's scurrilous poems, their status was changed – they became a considered insult to established social norms.

A more ambiguous case is supplied by the prints made by the artists who worked at Fontainebleau for François I and his successors. Some of these simply reproduced the compositions of the frescoes. Others, while using the same apparatus, push eroticism much further – as large-scale decorations they would clearly have been considered extremely indecorous, even by the standards of an openly libertine court.

The prints, being intended for private contemplation, can push matters much further towards the explicit than their public counterpart. The long tradition of mythological art offers the spectacle of a carefully calculated balancing act. The fact that it was sustained for five centuries, simultaneously satisfying the erotic impulse and at the same time denying some aspects of it, demonstrates both the irresistible attraction of the material and its potentially explosive nature within a society whose feelings about sexuality, derived from two opposed traditions, were not merely intensely ambiguous, but no less intense because of their ambiguity.

Once the tradition of classical learning which sustained this kind of art had broken down, erotic material in both art and literature became much more difficult to deal with successfully in the social sphere, and also in the purely artistic one.

*' She laid her fingers on his manly cheek,*
*The Gods' pure sceptres, and the darts of Love,*
*That with their touch might make a tiger meek,*
*Or might great Atlas from his seat remove;*
*So white, so soft, so delicate, so sleek,*
*As she had worn a lily for a glove,*
*As might beget life, where was never none*
*And put a spirit into the hardest stone. '*

MICHAEL DRAYTON *1563–1631*
THE BARON'S WARS, CANTO SIX

BELOW: *Boucher's rival* **Jean-Baptiste Greuze** *here tackles a typical Boucher subject in* Le Bain de Diane. *The chaste goddess of the hunt and her attendant nymphs occur frequently in Western art as an excuse to portray a group of female nudes.*

'*It is a kind of pleasing thing,*
*A pricking and a piercing sting.*'

ANONYMOUS *17th century*

BELOW: *It was socially unacceptable for women artists to paint erotic subjects in the nineteenth century. However,* **Berthe Morisot's** *(1811–95) depiction of Apollo visiting* Leto (Apollon visitant Latona, d'après Boucher) *was well received due to its mythical content and because she had copied the work of an Old Master.*

ABOVE: *This titillating*
*interpretation of* Leda and
the Swan, *attributed to*
**Charles-Antoine Coypel**
*(1694–1752), shows Zeus as*
*human from the waist down,*
*rather than wholly a bird.*

ABOVE: *In* **Scott Seidman's**
Baptism, 1993, *the pouring
on of water is shown as an
intimate, slow, loving gesture
rather than a brisk dunking.*

BELOW: *In this startling image,* The Masturbating Saint, 1995, *the artist* **Scott Seidman** *confronts the spectator with a vision of ecstasy: but is it spiritual transfiguration or sublime physical bliss?*

## Sonnet or Ditty

' *Mars in a fury 'gainst love's brightest Queen,*
*Put on his helm and took him to his lance;*
*On Erycinus mount was Mavors seen,*
*And there his ensigns did the god advance;*
*And by Heaven's great gates he stoutly swore,*
*Venus should die, for she had wronged him sore.*

*Cupid heard this and he began to cry,*
*And wished his mother's absence for a while:*
*"Peace, fool," quoth Venus, "is it I must die?*
*Must it be Mars?" With that, she coined a smile:*
*She trimmed her tresses and did curl her hair,*
*And made her face with beauty passing fair.*

*A fan of silver feathers in her hand,*
*And in a coach of ebony she went:*
*She passed the place where furious Mars did stand,*
*And out her looks a lovely smile she sent;*
*Then from her brows leaped out so sharp a frown,*
*That Mars for fear threw all his armour down.*'

*He vowed repentance for his rash misdeed.*
*Blaming his choler that had caused his woe;*
*Venus grew gracious, and with him agreed,*
*But charged him not to threaten beauty so,*
*For women's looks are such enchanting charms,*
*As can subdue the greatest god in arms.*

R O B E R T   G R E E N E
*1 5 5 8 – 9 2*
TULLIE'S LOVE 1589

## From Pan and Echo

*' Pan, hairy-thighed and goat-footed*
*Roaming the valleys and foothills*
*Low down on Olympus, need*
*Stiffening his prick, clouding*
*His barin, each emission*
*A momentary release*
*From the bondage of Eros…*

*Where is he now? I see him,*
*In sunlight, flexing his thighs*
*At Mediterraenean*
*Street corners. His nymhs descend*
*Giggling from aeroplanes, their*
*Ice-chip eyes scanning the locals*
*in search of the ultimate*
*Orgasm. These are easy lays who*
*Drive hard bargains.*

*Oh Echo!*
*Echo! He pursues you in markets,*
*He exposes his parts by the roadside. Every time*
*Your eye falls on that blunt paw*
*Groping his fly, your own thighs*
*Moisten. Turn away quickly,*
*Don your sunglasses, haggle*
*For tourist pots. You know he*
*Is watching still. '*

EDWARD LUCIE-SMITH

ABOVE: Leda and the Horses, 1993. A novel image of Leda by **Scott Seidman**. She is usually shown coupling with Zeus in the form of a swan, but is here seen with horses; perhaps there is to be a liaison with Poseidon, Zeus's brother, who often manifested himself as a lustful stallion.

ABOVE: The Love of Paris and Helen (1789) was painted by **Jacques-Louis David** just prior to the French Revolution for the Comte d'Artois, Louis XVI's notoriously immoral brother. David became a member of the Convention and voted for the death of the king.

RIGHT: *This is one of numerous images of lovers* by **George Grosz** *(1895–1959) executed in the Weimar period. Amants of 1923 is typical in its use of the artist and his wife as the picture's subjects.*

# D o w n   t o
# E A R T H

*n*on-mythological representations of the act of love have been problematical in almost all cultures, but perhaps most of all in a Western context. There are times and places, it is true, where frank, completely unmediated images of coition have had a religious significance. Some small sculptures of couples copulating are known from the Neolithic period, and a few of the great Indian temples of the medieval period are adorned, as has already been said, with sculptured friezes showing couples, and indeed groups, copulating in every imaginable position. In Ancient Greek and Roman art, however, the frank representation of the act of love, without some kind of mythological gloss, occurs in general only on minor art works: Greek vases and cups, Roman lamps, and occasional pieces of Roman silver show scenes of this sort. The intention seems to have been for the most part ironic or satiric.

In Eastern cultures, those of India, China and Japan, there was, at least until quite recently, a continuous tradition of making erotic paintings and prints. These were clearly for private study, not for public display. Some idea of their traditional usage, and also of the feelings the audience had about them, can be gained from the Chinese erotic novel *The Carnal Prayer Mat* by Li Yu, first published in 1634. In this, the protagonist uses an illustrated treatise on love to break down the resistance of a reluctant bride. The young woman is at first horrified:

' " I cannot quite believe that what the book represents is really compatible with morality and reason. If that were so, why did our forebears who created our social order not teach us to carry on openly, in broad daylight, before the eyes of strangers? Why do people do it like thieves in the night, shut away in their bedchambers? Doesn't that prove that the whole thing must be wrong and forbidden?"

The Before Midnight Scholar replied with a hearty laugh. "What a comical way of looking at things! But far be it from me to find fault with my niang-tzu, my dear little woman, on that account. It's all the fault of the preposterous way your father raised you, shutting you up in the house and cutting you off from the outside world, forbidding you to associate with young girls like yourself who could have enlightened you. Why, you've grown up like a hermit without the slightest knowledge of the world. Of course married couples conduct their business by day as well as night; everyone does. Just think for a moment; if it had never been done in daylight with others looking on, how would an artist have found out about all the different positions shown in this book? How could he have depicted all those forms and variations of loving union so vividly that one look at his pictures is enough to put you in a fine state of excitement?"

"Yes, but what about my parents? Why didn't they do it in the daytime?"

"I beg your pardon. How do you know that they didn't?" '[1]

This series of exchanges puts most of the problem in a nutshell, and is the more striking because it comes from a culture without the Judaeo-Christian concept of Original Sin. The sexual impulse, which is in one aspect an instinct for the survival of the human race, is probably the most powerful known to man. Its mainspring, the thing that drives it forward, is undoubtedly pleasure. This pleasure is, however, so intense that it produces the strongest possible negative reactions. It also produces the idea that the impulse must in some way be bridled, otherwise the

1. Li Yu. *The Carnal Prayer Mat* (Wordsworth Editions Limited, Ware, Hertfordshire, England, 1955) pp. 31–2.

whole of society will fall to pieces. Even within the institution of marriage, the Church's teaching has largely been that coition must be strictly for procreative, not for purely self-indulgent purposes.

Given the power of these feelings about the act of love, it seems only to be expected that most societies should have tried to control both descriptions of it, and still more so representations of it, often by draconian means. The result has often been a series of anomalies. Let me offer one small recent example, interesting in this context because it contrasts the present state of things in East and West in an interesting and unexpected way.

Let me begin with the proposition, which, I think most people interested in the field will accept, that it has often been easier to publish such material in the West if it came in suitably exotic guise. Hence, for instance, the publication of translations of the *1001 Nights* and the *Kama Sutra* in the nineteenth century were only semi-clandestine. Both of them were the work of the great traveller and scholar Sir Richard Burton (1821–1890), whose own erotic diaries were destroyed immediately after his death by his puritanical wife. Where the visual arts are concerned, the conventions and stylizations employed by Eastern artists have permitted publication in a Western context.

In 1995, the British Museum held a comprehensive exhibition of the art of Utamaro (1753–1806), one of the greatest of the Japanese *ukiyo-e* printmakers. Utamaro devoted his art almost entirely to life in the *yoshiwara* of the brothel quarter in Edo, as the Japanese capital was then called. No aspect of what took place there escaped him. Its existence is a well-established fact of Japanese social history. Among the images Utamaro produced were collections of *shunga* or erotic prints, showing geishas and their clients engaged in sexual intercourse. These print-series ostensibly served the same purpose as the illustrated erotic books described by Li Yu, that is, they were for the instruction and enlightenment of the uninitiated. Certainly they achieved a fairly wide circulation when they were made in the late eighteenth century.

As an integral part of Utamaro's achievement, all the artist's known *shunga* were included in the British Museum exhibition, which was booked for a later showing in Japan itself. However, in Utamaro's country of origin, it was agreed that the erotic subjects would have to be omitted.

Obviously the story opens some strange cultural and psychological perspectives. They become stranger still when one recalls some of the acts of sexual violence now depicted in contemporary Japanese *manga* or comic books, a form of publication which enjoys a vast circulation there, and whose conventions have even been adopted for educational purposes, since they are the preferred reading of many students.

If one tries to look at erotic representations featuring couples in a strictly Western context one is soon able to reach certain conclusions. First, while all such representations are traditionally regarded as explosive and socially dangerous, there are frequently mitigating

BELOW: **Stefan May** uses a close-up viewpoint and cropping to convey the urgent intensity of desire which is at once a cliché of romantic fiction and an overwhelming sensation shared by real lovers.

ABOVE: **Zsuzsi Roboz** *was
a pupil of Annigoni. Passion,
a 1997 pastel study, shows
an amplitude of form
derived from the classic
Italian tradition.*

'*As I plow, then harrow,
I turn around the sod.
I turn around my girl,
As I search that tiny hole.*'

SEX SONGS OF THE ANCIENT LETTS
TRS. BUD BERZING

75

ABOVE: *These energetic lovers, depicted c. 1970 by an Indian artist from Bundi in southeastern Rajasthan, combine two poses from the Kama Sutra.*

circumstances. One is the use of the elaborate mythological apparatus described in the last chapter, or the presence of exotic, non-Western elements as described in this one. Another, obviously, is the exact stage the lovers appear to have reached. Rodin's celebrated sculpture *The Kiss* (1886), for instance, has been on public display since the moment of its creation, even though both lovers are nude, and there is no pretence that this is a mythological incident.

In general, a 'protective' element has always been the celebrity of the artist. Thus there has been a reluctance to suppress representations of lovers by eighteenth-century artists such as Fragonard, or even twentieth-century ones like Picasso (1881–1973), even when it was obvious that full sexual intercourse was the thing depicted. Another protective element has sometimes been the fact that the images, rather than being meant for full public display, were on a small scale. Illustrations in books, such as the British artist Michael Ayrton's (1921–76) superb illustrations of Paul Verlaine's erotic poems, have escaped the kind of censure that might have been attracted by paintings that attempted to express the same subject-matter.

The established quality of the literary text has also tended not merely to defend that text itself, but any illustrations an artist might care to make. Verlaine (1844-96) is one of the great names of nineteenth-century French literature, and anything he wrote is therefore of interest. One point is nevertheless worth making; the poems in question deal with homosexual as well as heterosexual coition, and Ayrton provided illustrations for one species of poem quite as vigorously and candidly as he did the other.

This is a relatively new development. Until the second half of the twentieth century homosexual representations were doubly forbidden: for showing the act of love, and for showing it taking place between males. Ayrton is only one of a number of twentieth-century artists to break through this barrier. Another is David Hockney, whose sequence of drawings *Waking Up* does not even offer the excuse of being text illustrations.

ABOVE: *In this fifth-century BC red figure vase painting, a bearded athlete takes a young woman from behind. The rather androgynous girl is typical of those portrayed in Greek vase scenes.*

The same prohibition has not applied historically to images of lesbians making love to one another. Such representations, sometimes with mythological precedent (the legend of Jupiter and Callisto) but also sometimes without it (as in some Fontainebleau School paintings of women bathing together), have been an established part of the repertoire since the sixteenth century. One reason for this is that lesbian erotica appeals to males, without threatening their self-image, as homosexual erotica seems to do. Courbet's (1819–77) famous painting *Le Sommeil* (1866), one of the most forthright lesbian images produced by a great artist, was painted by a heterosexual painter for a heterosexual male client, an Egyptian Bey.

Today the situation is extremely complicated. The stripping away of the whole traditional cultural apparatus means that, more than ever, the audience has to take

RIGHT: All Passion Spent –
The Satisfied Woman *is a*
shunga *print from around*
*1855 by one of the last*
*great* ukiyo-e *artists,*
**Kuniyoshi** *(1798–1861).*
*A strong influence of*
*Western art can be seen.*

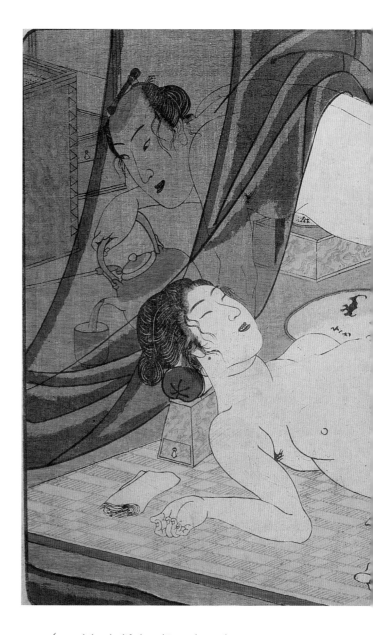

representations of the act of love as something literally intended. This is even more strongly the case with photography, as the photographic image, as we have already seen, always carries the implication, though thanks to recent technological advances now sometimes deceptively, that what is represented actually happened. These are the things which particularly preoccupy the feminist lobby. If one believes that all representations of the nude female are at least potentially exploitative, and part of a tradition of phallocratic exploitation of women, then one must certainly object still more strongly to any image which shows the female actually being penetrated by the male. Similar objections apply, in a slightly more distanced way, to images of lesbian sex, since these are known to be of interest to heterosexual males. Feminist arguments do, however, leave the situation concerning hard-core homosexual images unclear, since it is hard to see how any argument concerning the exploitation of women can be stretched far enough to apply to these. The situation has in fact, in a strictly feminist context, been turned topsy-turvy. What was least permissible, is now (logic indicates) what is most permissible.

One result of this seems to be an increasingly violent collision between feminism and avant-gardism, though in the visual arts these two impulses were until recently thought to be in some way allied. Yet the original twentieth-century avant-garde was often violently misogynistic, much more so than the Impressionist and Symbolist generations which immediately preceded it. One does not have to look very far to discover misogynistic phrases in Italian Futurist manifestos.

*'…and then he lifted my hips and turned me*
*so that I was on my back, my legs over the side of*
*the bed, bent at the knee, and he kneeled on the*
*floor, his fingers inside of me, too, hooked deep inside,*
*the way a man carries something hooked on*
*a finger over his shoulder, and he sucked my clitoris*
*into his mouth. There was nothing intervening.*
*Not even a nightgown. Not even a penis.*
*"Come all over me", he said. '*

SUSANNA MOORE
IN THE CUT 1995

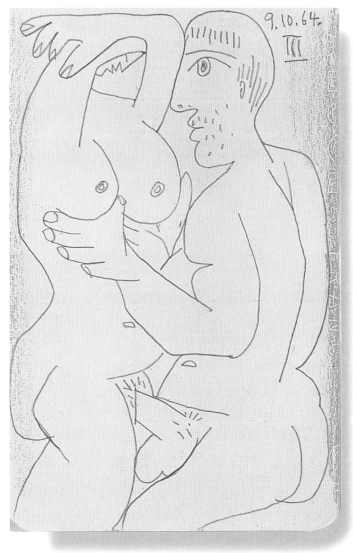

RIGHT: **Picasso** *executed erotic drawings throughout his career. Couple, dated 9 October 1964, has an erotic poignancy resulting from its extreme simplicity.*

ABOVE: Couple Embracing by **Stefan May** close-in and cropped in his trademark style; this time, it's Girls on Top with the focus on the breasts.

BELOW: **Stefan May** *here has adopted his usual compositional technique of cropping to enhance the eroticism in the image of* *the couple embracing. The spectator focuses on the man's face resting upon the woman's breast.*

'*...and then he lifted my hips...*'

SUSANNA MOORE
IN THE CUT 1995

The Futurists, like many other artists of the same generation, were inspired by Friedrich Nietzsche (1844–1900), who envisaged the creation of an *übermensch*, with strong emphasis on the masculine gender.

In a climate where the avant-garde has become an increasingly official manifestation, it has been hard for artists to discover attitudes, and images to reflect these attitudes, which would genuinely challenge the status quo. Jeff Koons' sanctification of the conventions of blue-collar mass-market pornography is as much a rebellion against a kind of 'every right thinking person agrees' liberal consensus as it is a gesture of defiance made against political authority.

Where words are concerned, as opposed to images, it increasingly looks as if we live in a society where everything is permitted.

## she being Brand

' she being Brand

-new; and you
know consequently a
little stiff i was
careful of her and (having

thoroughly oiled the universal
joint tested my gas felt of
her radiator made sure her springs were O

K.) i went right to it flooded-the-carburettor cranked her
up, slipped the
clutch (and then somehow got into reverse she
kicked what
the hell) next
minute i was back in neutral tried and

again slo-wly; barely nudg. ing (my

lev-er Right-
oh and her gears being in
AI shape passed
from low through
second-in-to-the high like
greasedlightning) just as we turned the corner of Divinity

avenue i touched the accelerator and give

her the juice, good
            (it
was the first ride and believe i we was
happy to see how nice she acted right up to
the last minute coming back down by the Public
Gardens i slammed on
the

internalexpanding
&
externalcontracting
brakes Bothatonce and

brought allofher tremB
-ling
to a : dead.

stand-
;Still) '

e . e . c u m m i n g s
1 8 9 4 – 1 9 6 2

ABOVE: *Leading US feminist artist* **Judy Chicago** *is one of relatively few to represent female sexuality in art. In her 1975 piece,* Sex from the Inside Out, *Chicago utilized the medium of china paint on china.*

BELOW: *The title image from* **Judy Chicago's** Sex from the Inside Out, *a witty 'cunt's eye view' of the sexual act.*

ABOVE: *Eroticism in the traditional style continued to be painted in India throughout the nineteenth century. Increasingly, as seen in these lovers painted in Rajasthan at the turn of this century, they showed the growing influence of Western art on established traditions.*

' *"Christ you are a marvelous girl!"*
*That took her breath away. "Oh, am I?*
*"Yes!"*
*"Am I ?"*
*"Yes! Yes! Yes! Now can I fuck you?"*
*" Oh, sweetheart, darling," cried The Monkey,*
*"pick a hole, any hole, I'm yours!"* '

PHILIP ROTH
PORTNOY'S COMPLAINT 1969

BELOW: *In* Lovers, *a* *is initially unclear. The*
shunga *print from* The *Japanese considered th*
Poem of the Pillow, *exposed nape of a*
**Utamaro** *has entwined his* *woman's neck, seen he*
*lovers so that their position* *to be particularly eroti*

BELOW: *The unusual setting of* Lovers in a Tent, *engraved by* **Eric Gill** *in 1929, combined with the artist's stringent draughtsmanship, gives the image a special erotic piquancy.*

RIGHT: *It is interesting to note the role of the woman as sexual aggressor in this erotic Roman relief from Pompeii. However she is a 'working girl.'*

'But Deadeye Dick would not come quick,
He meant to conserve his powers,
When in the mind he'd grind and grind
For more than a couple of hours.

She lay a while with a subtle smile
And then her grip grew keener,
And with a sigh she sucked him dry
With the ease of a vacuum cleaner.

.She did this feat in a way so neat
As to set at grand defiance
The primary cause of the basic laws
That govern all sexual science.

She simply rode that phallic tool,
That for years had stood the test,
And accepted rules of the ancient schools
In a second or two went west!'

ANONYMOUS *20th century*
ESKIMO NELL

ABOVE: *In contrast to comparatively fantastic French eroticism of the same period, Hungarian artist* **Mihaily von Zichy** *(1827–1906) produced many frank erotic illustrations such as* A Man and a Woman Making Love, *used in the 1911* Liebe.

ABOVE: *Grave, respectful, focused; lovers behaving well in this erotic photograph which manages to avoid most of the clichés of the genre.*

RIGHT: *This image by* **Elke Selzle** *gives a sense of absolute immediacy; it is as if the spectator were physically present, sharing the moment of abandon.*

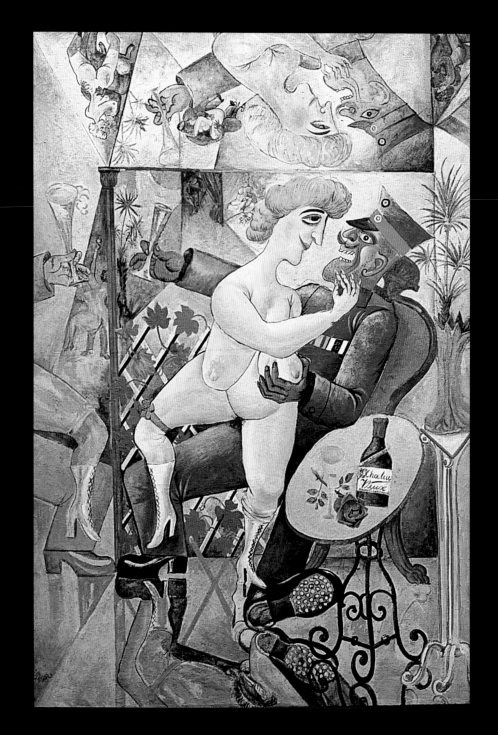

ABOVE: *A World War I German soldier entertains a Belgian prostitute in* Souvenir de la galerie des glaces à Bruxelles, *painted in 1920 by* **Otto Dix.**

*'Ye Gods! the raptures of that night!*
*What fierce convulsions of delight!*
*How in each other's arms involv'd,*
*We lay confounded, and dissolv'd!*
*Bodies mingling, sexes blending,*
*Which should most be lost contending;*
*Darting fierce, and flaming kisses,*
*Plunging into boundless blisses;*
*Our bodies and our souls on fire,*
*Tost by a tempest of desire;*
*'Till with the utmost fury dow'n,*
*Down, at once, we sunk to heav'n.'*

ANONYMOUS
*19th century*

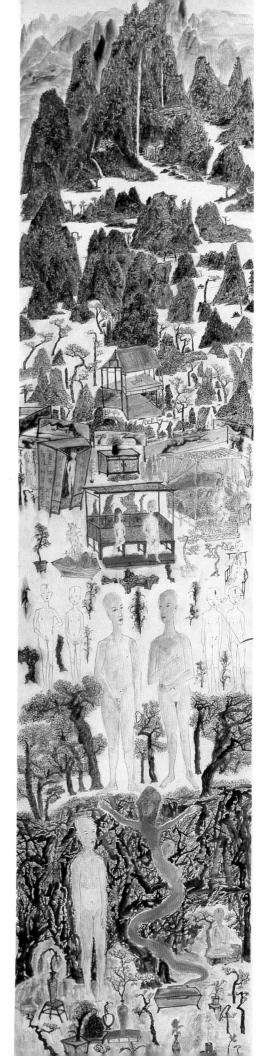

RIGHT: **Yu Peng's** *1990 painting,* Working for a Living, *takes an ironic look at the relationship between men and women, particularly the female role.*

91

ABOVE: *Of all the French eighteenth-century artists,* **Fragonard** *was the most candid about sex. Like Boucher, he portrays extremely youthful lovers. Those seen in* The Moment Desired *or* The Happy Lovers *are barely out of childhood.*

BELOW: *These two haunting images were made by* **Evelyn Williams** *in 1996.* Togetherness I *(bottom picture) and* Togetherness II, *as well as being formal exercises in flesh tones, line and form, are also depictions of post-coital tristesse. Although the lovers are physically entwined, their expressions indicate that emotionally they are separate entities.*

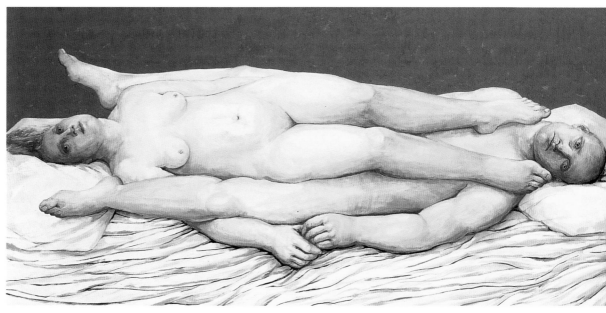

# LOOKING *on*

*a*ny erotic representation implies the presence of an onlooker. In the sense that the spectator is the onlooker – the conjunction of the erotic image and the person looking at it already amounts to an act of voyeurism. What is perhaps surprising in the history of erotic art in general is the presence of an onlooker within the composition, who acts as a transitional element, a point of identification. The myth or story which makes the point most directly when presented in pictorial form is the biblical tale of Susannah. Tintoretto's superb *Susannah and the Elders* (c. 1556) in the Kunsthistorisches Museum in Vienna is the paradigm of the voyeuristic impulse; the female nude nestles within the generally dark tonality of the picture like a shining baroque pearl. Her glistening nudity seems to be actually illuminated by the lustful glances of the males who look at her as if caught in the beam of a theatrical spotlight. Tintoretto's use of brilliantly effective, totally non-naturalistic lighting schemes is seldom better demonstrated than here, in what is considered to be one of his masterpieces.

Tintoretto (1518–94) is not alone among the great Venetians of the sixteenth century in making use of onlookers as a focus for the spectator's own voyeurism.

### Miss Twye

*'Miss Twye was soaping her breasts in her bath*
*When she heard behind her a meaning laugh*
*And to her amazement she discovered*
*A wicked man in the bathroom cupboard.'*

GAVIN EWART *1916–1993*

*Venus and Cupid with an Organ Player*, one of the works painted for Philip II by Titian, is an especially blatant example. Rather than peering from behind a curtain, as such onlookers frequently do, the young musician is seated at the foot of the couch upon which Venus herself reclines, either unconscious of or quite indifferent to his scrutiny. He has turned from his instrument, whose clustering pipes have phallic implications in themselves, and looks directly at her crotch. The angle at which both figures are placed ensures that, while we who look at the painting cannot see the goddess' sexual parts in all their detail, it is nevertheless clear that the organ player can. He examines Venus' sexuality on our behalf.

This is in fact an unusually forthright image, not merely for its own time, but for any time or place. As a number of passages in *My Secret Life* tell us, one of the excitements of voyeurism is not merely the idea of seeing what is normally kept hidden, but that of seeing it unknown to the actual participants.

Walter describes watching through the keyhole while a young English couple copulate in a Paris hotel room next to his own:

'Then peeping out of my door, for I had an intense desire to get near her, to gloat upon her, I watched them go downstairs to the *table d'hôte* room, and following seated myself as near as I could to them. I watched her while she ate her breakfast, scarcely able to keep my eyes off her. I fancied I saw her with his prick moving up and down her cunt between her fair round bum cheeks, and her thigh up in the air, held there, by his arm, and who would have thought that that sweet, modest looking woman would have cocked her leg up so like a well paced harlot, or that the fingers of that quiet man buttering his bread, had half an hour before been bathing them in his wife's cunt.'[1]

1. Walter, *My Secret Life*, Vol II (Arrow Books Limited, London, 1994) p. 205.

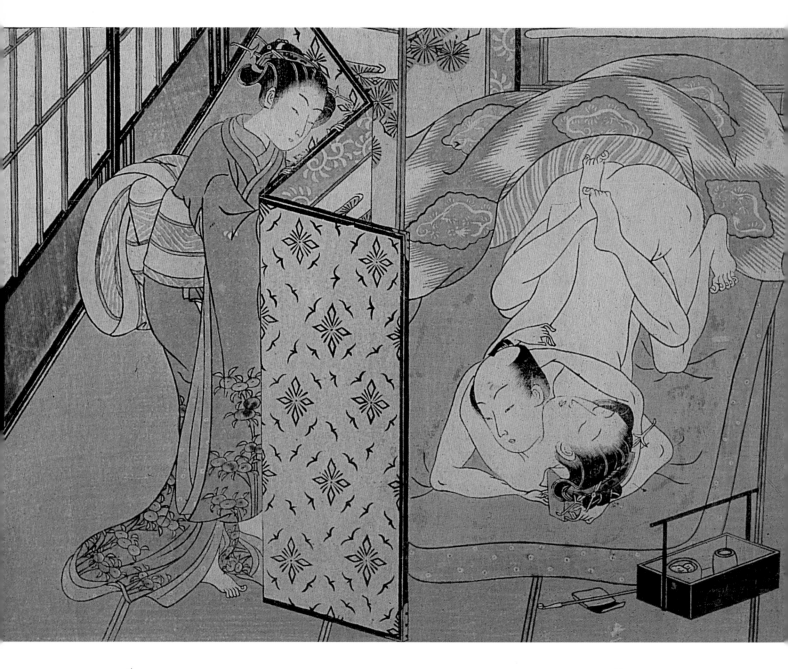

'Now and then the
man placed his hand over
her head as if to restrain
her frenzy.'

ANAÏS NIN 1903–77
THE WOMAN ON THE DUNES

ABOVE: *Voyeurism is a
frequent theme in Japanese
art. Here* Isoda Koryusai
*(fl.1765–84) depicts lovers lost
in lust observed by a maid.*

A little later, having divined that the wife at least is aware of the keyhole he has been using to spy through, he decides to give her a show of his own:

> ' I pushed a chair to such a spot, that lolling in it I could see light through the keyhole, took up a newspaper, and seeming to read it, held it so that I could look over its edge at the keyhole. Soon the keyhole darkened for some minutes. All that time I kept my prick stiff so that she might see it well, and felt great delight in the idea of her having seen another prick stiff besides her husband's. Would she tell her husband? I wondered, – and did she? Most likely not. – Did I make her lewd? It is quite possible. '[2]

Among the erotic artists who show a particular fascination with voyeuristic situations are the designers of Japanese *shunga*. Their ingenuity in devising situations where the lovers can be watched is almost limitless. Servants listen at doorways, or peer from behind screens. The Japanese printmakers are also extremely ingenious in creating designs which imply a voyeuristic element. Sometimes, for instance, the participant couple are half-veiled by a mosquito net. Sometimes the image of their amatory endeavours is reflected in a mirror.

These situations and devices find their equivalents, though usually not in quite such elegant form, in many of the erotic prints of the eighteenth and early nineteenth centuries. These, too, make the point that exhibitionistic and voyeuristic impulses are closely linked.

One of the most effective tools of the contemporary voyeur is of course the camera. Indeed, as Susan Sontag and other modern theoreticians of photography have implied, the medium is inherently voyeuristic, and implies, in addition, that the photographer not merely witnesses the thing he points his lens at but, through his or her ability to record what is seen, actually takes possession of the event. The situation has been pushed still further through the rapid progress of technology. The polaroid camera and the video camera make the recorded image instantly available, and this immediacy can, if required, become part of a sexual transaction. The participants can admire their own performance almost at

ABOVE: *In* The Moorish Bath *by* **Jean Leon Gerôme** *the naked beauty invites the voyeurism of the spectator, as well as her attendants.*

the very moment when the performance itself is taking place. At the same time, because the image does not have to be processed, people who use these devices feel that their erotic privacy is compromised only to the extent that they themselves wish it to be.

The digital camera, which feeds visual images directly to a computer, is now, as users of the Internet are aware, having a slightly different, and perhaps in the long run even more radical effect, by making certain forms of exhibitionism possible on a global scale. A man (most often it is a man) with exhibitionist impulses can now display his penis anonymously to an audience of tens of thousands, and perhaps even hundreds of thousands. And once fed in the system, such an image completely escapes

2. Ibid., p. 207.

ABOVE: In **Hugues Taraval's**
(1729–85) Le bat the model
points to a packhorse in the
painting on the easel, whilst
the young artist's attention is
transfixed elsewhere.

the control of the person who originally created it; even the actual file-name which identifies it can be changed at will by anyone who cares to download. Such images do not degenerate with time, and can be replicated with no degradation of quality.

Home-made erotica of the kind I am talking about here does not necessarily qualify as 'art', though it is notorious that the boundaries between art and not-art have in the late twentieth century become increasingly difficult to define. Yet they must surely change the artistic context, and in particular our notion of what is or isn't permitted. It is no good making rules, or enacting laws, when they are self-evidently unenforceable.

What this implies is that modern erotica increasingly comes into sharp collision with an established tradition of privacy. The still camera, the video camera and now the electronic media make the boundaries between what takes place in private and what takes place in public increasingly precarious and difficult to maintain. Is this something totally novel, or does it mean that we are gradually reverting to the situation which existed before the so-called 'modern' world came into being? Privacy, as a concept, was invented by the aristocracy of the late Middle Ages, who retreated from the common hall to a private room called the solar. In the hands of monarchs, the idea was further elaborated. One of the fascinations of visiting Loches, a French royal residence of the early fifteenth century which has retained more or less its original form, is to see that it consists essentially of a very large and elaborate fortification surrounding a small and simple house, the *logis royaux*. This has a big hall, and behind that a bedchamber and a couple of small cabinets or dressing rooms. Only in these few rooms reserved to himself was the monarch not on public show.

Later, at Versailles, in the time of Louis XIV and his immediate successors, the monarchs led schizophrenic lives. There was the state bedroom, where the king was ceremonially dressed and undressed, and there were the tiny private rooms tucked away behind the scenes, where he led his real, non-ceremonial life. By that time, of course, the

ABOVE: *An exhausted goddess, abandoned in sleep, unwakeable even by the chattering putti, lies oblivious to the passing peasant in this picture by an anonymous artist in the style of Titian.*

' *Who sees his true-love in her naked bed,*
*Teaching the sheets a whiter hue than white,*
*But when his glutton eye so full hath fed,*
*His other agents aim at like delight?*
*Who is so faint that dares not be so bold,*
*To touch the fire the weather being cold?* '

WILLIAM SHAKESPEARE
*1564–1616*
VENUS AND ADONIS

modern bourgeoisie had come into being and had given the idea of privacy its present moral overtone. Practically all physical functions, and especially those which had anything to do with sex, became matters for shame and therefore concealment. The voyeur's thrill comes from the sense of transgression which he, or she, derives from violating a taboo. The sense of privacy became one of the things that distinguished humanity from the beasts.

This is one of the reasons, I suspect, why European explorers and traders persecuted 'naked' tribesmen so vigorously. The Indians of Tierra del Fuego, who had never learned the use of clothes, despite the severity of the climate, were considered by Darwin to be 'lower than dogs'. Today the situation is complicated not merely by the fact that privacy has become more difficult to sustain but also by the way in which it is deliberately challenged. Increasingly it is a point of pride to possess a beautiful body, and such a possession is meant to be displayed. Does the concept of the voyeur have any continuing validity in the day of the nudist beach and the see-through blouse? To open the door to voyeurism is, in a sense, to invalidate the concept of it altogether.

BELOW: **Balthus** *(b. 1908) represents the spectator's gaze with light in* Nude with a Cat. *The erotically posed young nude is spotlit as her attendant opens a window.*

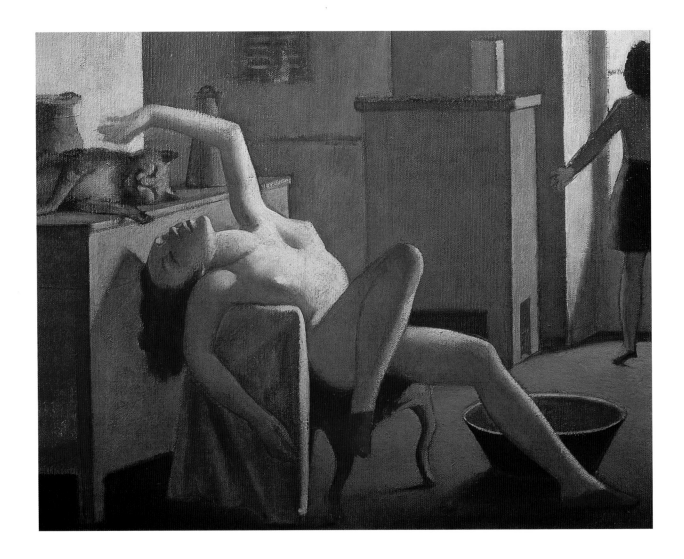

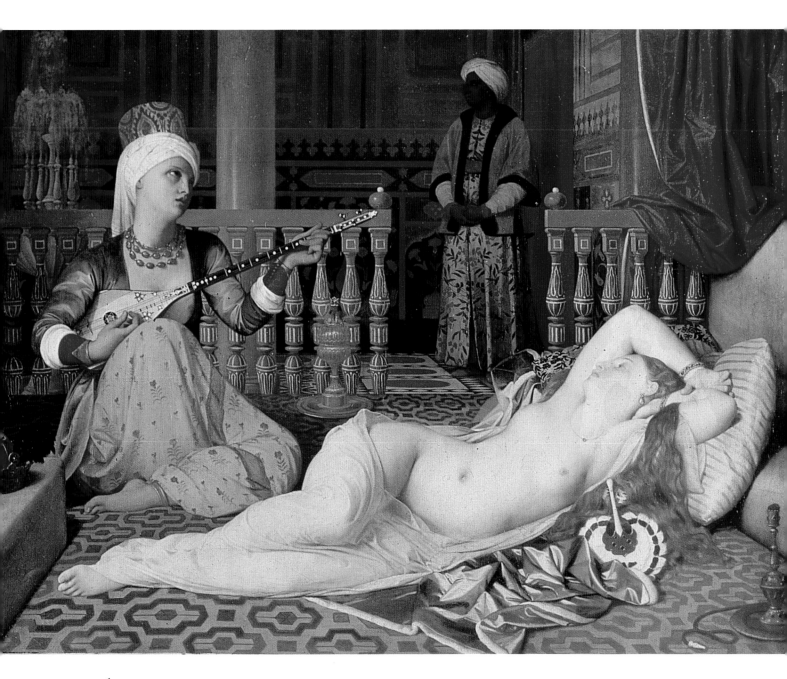

‘ *Who sees his true-love*
*in her naked bed...* ’

WILLIAM SHAKESPEARE  *1564–1616*
VENUS AND ADONIS

ABOVE: J.A.D. Ingres'
*harem beauty immodestly*
*exposes herself to her*
*attendants in* Odalisque
with a Slave, *painted*
*between 1836 and 1840.*

' Then he saw that one of the cottages was lighted.
It was set into the woods, isolated.
It intrigued him that anyone should be up
so late. He approached it soundlessly, his
footsteps lost in the sand. The Venetian blinds were
down but not tightly closed, so
he could see right into the room. And his eyes met
the most amazing sight: a very
wide bed, profusely covered with pillows and
rumpled blankets, as if it had already
been the scene of a great battle; a man, seemingly
cornered in a pile of pillows, as if
pushed there after a series of attacks,
reclining like a pasha in a harem, very calm and
contented, naked, his legs folded out; and a woman,
also naked, whom Louis could
see only from the back, contorting herself before this
pasha, undulating and deriving
such pleasure from whatever she was doing with her
head between his legs that her
ass would shake tremulously, her legs
tighten as if she were about to leap.

Now and then the man placed his hand over her
head as if to restrain her frenzy.
He tried to move away. Then she leaped
with great agility and placed herself over
him, kneeling over his face. He no longer
moved. His face was directly under her
sex, which, her stomach curved outwards,
she held before him.

As he was pinned under her, she was the
one to move within reach of his mouth,
which had not touched her yet. Louis saw
the man's sex rise and lengthen, and he
tried with an embrace to bring her down
upon him. But she remained at a short
distance, looking, enjoying the spectacle of
her own beautiful stomach and hair and
sex so near to his mouth.

Then slowly, slowly she moved towards
him and, with her head bowed, watched the
melting of his mouth between her legs. '

ANAÏS NIN *1903–77*
THE WOMAN ON THE DUNES

ABOVE: **He Duoling's** Rear
Window, No. 3 of 1996
*provides a contemporary*

*ironic view of traditional
Chinese and Japanese
voyeuristic compositions.*

ABOVE: Undercovercop: The Coefficients of Desire, 1974. **Jack Fritscher's** edgy photograph presents the object of homosexual desire as both the observer and the thing observed. The air of menace is palpable.

‘ *But she remained at a short distance, looking...* ’

ANAÏS NIN *1903–77*
THE WOMAN ON THE DUNES

ABOVE: *The Old Testament story of Susannah and the Elders is the quintessential paradigm of voyeurism. The subject has been used frequently in painting by a* wide variety of artists as a *vehicle for imaginative erotic compositions. A good example is* **Tintoretto's** Susannah Bathing, *painted from 1555 to 1556.*

BELOW: *Commissioned by Philip II of Spain,* Venus and Cupid with an Organ Player *is one of* **Titian's** *more candidly erotic paintings. The direction of the young musician's gaze is particularly poignant here.*

RIGHT: *An etching by* **Michael Ayrton** *illustrating* 'Il est Mauvais Coucheur' *('He's an Awkward Customer') by Paul Verlaine. Ayrton made 15 etchings for a limited edition of Verlaine's* Femmes/Hombres *published in 1972.*

# *Boys will be* BOYS

homosexual erotica featuring males *is* scarcely unknown, in the long history of art and literature, but it has until recently tended to be both rare and clandestine. Absolutely specific images of male–male sexual interaction occur, as is well known, on Greek vases. Usually they are courtship scenes, in which an older male addresses himself to a youth. This conforms to a well-known aspect of Greek culture, in which such relationships were considered to be in many ways superior, ethically and in terms of their contribution to society, to those between men and women. Where male–male sexual intercourse is shown in Greek art, it usually takes place intercrurally. Anal penetration, seen on a handful of vases, is almost invariably the business of the half-human satyr.

The Italian Renaissance saw the reappearance of homosexual imagery in art, but not usually the portrayal of males actually having sex together. A substantial number of the leading artists of the High Renaissance seem to have been homosexual by preference, as we know from the written record – among their number were Donatello, Michelangelo and Leonardo. Benvenuto Cellini was bisexual. At the end of his life he was under house arrest, accused of a homosexual assault on one of his pupils. Caravaggio also appears to have been bisexual,

> ' *He leaned back against the wall and the man leaned towards him, pushing his way further into David's mouth...* '
>
> OSCAR MOORE
> A MATTER OF LIFE AND SEX 1991

though some writers on his work have preferred to see him as being inclined more towards boys than to women. Surviving testimony, legal and anecdotal, shows him involved with a Roman prostitute, but also as fascinated with young boys. Typically the homosexual love object, at the time of the Renaissance, was an adolescent or a very young man, not an individual of mature years.

Paintings and sculptures with homosexual overtones, among them a number of very celebrated works, are almost invariably a celebration of the beauty of young males. Among them are two famous images of the biblical David, one in bronze by Donatello, and the other in marble by Michelangelo.

One reason why Caravaggio has, in our own time, become something of a hero figure in the homosexual community is the lack of idealization in his imagery; his models are palpably human and alive. Even when he places a nude boy in an allegorical context, as he does in the celebrated *Amore Vincitore* now in Berlin, the actual subject remains a recognizable Roman ragamuffin, who gives the spectator a peculiarly seductive look. The painting was commissioned from Caravaggio by a member of the aristocratic Giustiniani family, who is said to have kept the image concealed by a curtain, showing it only to favoured intimates. This seems to indicate that the image does indeed have a freight of secondary meanings.

> 'And his gorgeous dreamy arse, his
> Maddening, cunning, cocky, whoreish,
> Jesus-Christ-Almighty arse suddenly
> presses into my belly'

PAUL VERLAINE 1844–96

Similar ambiguities can be found in the European literature of the sixteenth and seventeenth centuries. For English-speakers, the most famous examples are some of Shakespeare's sonnets, especially this one:

'  A woman's face, with Nature's own hand painted,
Hast thou, the Master Mistress of my passion;
A woman's gentle heart, but not acquainted
With shifting change, as is false woman's fashion;
An eye more bright than theirs, less false in rolling,
Gilding the object whereupon it gazeth;
A man in hue all hues in his controlling,
Which steals men's eyes and women's souls amazeth.
And for a woman wert thou first created;
Till Nature, as she wrought thee, fell a-doting,
And by addition me of thee defeated
By adding one thing to my purpose nothing.
    But since she prick'd thee out for women's pleasure,
Mine be thy love, and thy love's use their treasure. '

The precise meaning of this, and even the question of whether it is addressed to a male or a female, though that the former is the case seems obvious from the text, has been violently debated. Is it a declaration of sexual attraction, or merely, as some have contended, a piece of flattery addressed to an aristocratic patron? Though it seems intolerable to many people that the English national poet should have harboured erotic feelings towards a member of his own sex, in many ways, and despite obfuscation on the part of the author himself, it seems to read most naturally and logically if we understand it as being addressed to another and almost certainly younger man.

On the whole this homosexual strain tended to re-surface in Western art whenever aspects of Greek culture came back into fashion.

There is, for example, a homoerotic strand in the Neo-Classical movement (Winckelmann, the founding theoretician of Neo-Classicism, was homosexual, and was robbed and murdered by one of his lovers). It is intermittently visible in the work of perhaps the most celebrated of all Neo-Classical artists, Jacques-Louis David, and most clearly of all in his *Leonidas*, a composition which preoccupied him for many years. David was a married man, with children, but his

LEFT AND BELOW: *Until recently, the representation of homosexual couples was the cause of much more controversy than their heterosexual equivalents. In* both of these untitled gay images, completed in 1997 by **Edward Lucie-Smith**, cropping has masked the identity of the lovers, leaving purely the sexual act defined.

## Sleepily Murmuring...,

'*Sleepily murmuring, not certain as yet what manner of pleasure this is, or if it is part of your dream or the waking to come, you turn, arrange yourself, and accept the sensation. And I, uncertain, not of the act, but whether I've been given permission to enter and mingle myself with what you are dreaming, advance like a child in a game, two steps forward, one back, until I am sure of a welcome. You open your eyes, suddenly, and I am caught out, stumble drown in the turbulent blue.*'

EDWARD LUCIE-SMITH

biography also shows that he had powerful emotional attachments to some of his male pupils.

The end of the nineteenth century and the opening years of the twentieth saw the resurgence of images, in both art and in literature, which can be described as homoerotic. But the period also witnessed a series of homosexual scandals: that connected with the name of Oscar Wilde in Britain, and another in Germany involving Prince Eulenberg, at one time an adviser to the Kaiser, and the circle surrounding him. These scandals occupy what now seems like a curious historical position: they mark the moment when homosexuality emerged as a new and self-consciously separate aspect of Western culture. Earlier scandals of the same type, like the millionaire William Beckford's liaison with a young aristocrat, do not seem to have had the same impact, though Beckford lost any hope of the peerage to which his wealth might have entitled him, and was forced to spend a long period abroad.

The history of homosexuality has been a matter of comparatively recent study. Research seems to demonstrate that, while homosexual acts certainly took place more or less throughout the entire history of Western society, self-identified homosexuals made a comparatively late appearance on the scene. In the England of Shakespeare's time, for example, exclusive homosexuality was rare, and bisexuality much closer to the norm among those attracted to their own sex - though the mother of the great philosopher Francis Bacon (1561–1626) reproached him vehemently in a letter for sleeping with his male servants. In the same period, James I, notorious for his attraction to handsome young men, fathered a number of children. It is only in the late seventeenth century that one first hears of so-called 'molly houses', and of homosexuals who identified one another through certain mannerisms and turns of phrase. Homosexual history is also complicated to an unusual extent by considerations of class. In nineteenth-century England and America, there seems to have been less inhibition over homosexual acts among young

BELOW: *This print of wrestlers by* **Rod Judkins** *stresses that gay relationships have a combative element. This theme was also tackled by* *Francis Bacon (1909–92) in his transformation of an Eadweard Muybridge photograph of nude wrestlers into a homosexual coupling.*

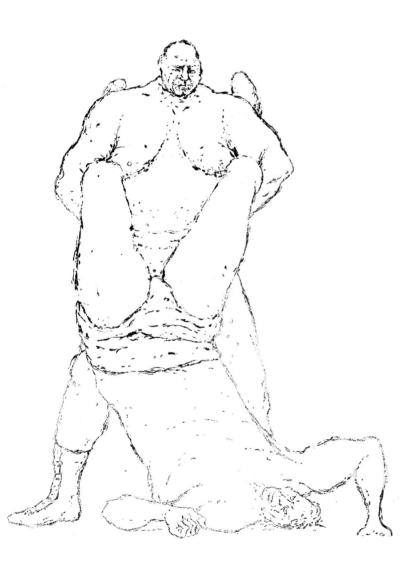

'*Best thieves within the bathhouse door,*
*Vibennius and his fairy son:*
*The quicker dad's hand is, the more*
*His son's ass fucks for everyone.*
*Go look for some queer country where*
*You wretches aren't known so well;*
*Here all know dad's light-fingered flair,*
*So sonny's hairy ass won't sell.* '

CATULLUS *C.84–C.54BC*

ABOVE: *A phallic contest,*
*from a* shunga *scroll. Oriental*
*attitudes towards homoerotica*
*are more relaxed than*
*those in the West.*

working-class males than was the case with those higher up the social scale. This can be confirmed from any reasonably close study of the life and work of Walt Whitman. In addition to this, working-class males often prostituted themselves for money. Until the early decades of this century, for example, soldiers of the elite Guards regiments in England often supplemented their pay in this fashion. The young soldiers who behaved in this way did not think of themselves as homosexual, and were not so identified by their clientele. This indeed was part of their very attraction.

BELOW: Sleepwalker (**Erich Fischl**), 1979. *At once suburban and surreal, a boy masturbates into his childhood's paddling pool.*

*Perhaps the artist is trying to reveal to the dreamer sexual proclivities that remain unacknowledged in waking hours.*

The gradual decriminalization of homosexuality, the so-called 'gay liberation' which took place at an increasingly accelerated pace in both Britain and the United States from the mid-1960s onwards, led to an increased production of homosexual erotica, and also to a startlingly abrupt and rapid change in both its nature and its status. In the United States in particular, material of this nature began to be seen as something which benefited from the constitutional guarantee of freedom of speech. Homosexual imagery diversified and altered. Previously the object of homosexual desire had been the juvenile athlete. Now a much wider range of erotic fantasy offered itself – the wished for partner could be the bodybuilder, the leatherman, the 'bear' or even the punk or skinhead. Material which had been strictly 'underground', like the photographs of Bruce of Los Angeles or the erotic drawings of Tom of Finland,

ABOVE: *One of* **Chris Nelson's** Bear Cult *series shows John and Joe* *serene and relaxed, lovers* *who have resisted any* *form of stereotyping.*

ABOVE: *The salacious illustrations to the 1896 edition of Aristophanes' bawdy play* Lysistrata, *by* **Aubrey Beardsley** *(1872–98), are some of his finest works.* The Examination of the Herald *adds a homosexual subtext to the heterosexual story.*

moved close to the artistic mainstream. The reputation of Wilhelm von Glöden (1856–1931) was revived, and his work was now seen as a serious contribution to the history of photography, as was the work of another homoerotic photographer of the same period, the American F. Holland Day. Robert Mapplethorpe (1946–89), in the late 1970s and early 1980s, succeeded in getting homosexual imagery of an extremely explicit kind accepted as a legitimate contribution to the American visual arts avant-garde. More significant even than this, Mapplethorpe's driving ambition was largely responsible for a change in attitude towards photography as a whole. What had till then been regarded as a separate field of artistic endeavour was now accepted as being one among a number of means of image-making, all with the same aesthetic status.

Following in Mapplethorpe's wake, photographers such as Bruce Weber and Herb Ritts made photographic images with strongly homoerotic overtones which became acceptable in magazine advertising and even on billboards. Striking campaigns of this sort were devised for major clothing labels such as Calvin Klein and Versace. Indeed, the use of the naked or near-naked male as a way to sell goods became less controversial than the employment of images showing women in a state of undress. The fact that the goods being sold were, more often than not, being marketed to men, and that the erotic allure of the imagery was therefore being directed to members of the same sex as the models, was now taken completely for granted.

Today homosexual imagery benefits from gay liberation's membership of the 'rainbow coalition' of recognition-seeking minorities which has come to dominate avant-garde art, and the visual arts in particular. There are, however, a number of divisions within the homosexual arts. The AIDS epidemic confirmed the status of the male homosexual as a member of an endangered species, and gave a tragic undercurrent to imagery which might otherwise have been purely hedonistic. A number of artists self-identified as AIDS

LEFT: *In* Two Men, *painted in 1996, British artist* **Harry Holland** *reveals the role weariness and anxiety play in homosexual relationships.*

activists, among them the late David Wojnarowicz (1954–92), used images borrowed from homosexual pornography in a deliberately aggressive way. Though certainly intended to be erotic in their original guise, these images hardly make an erotic effect in their new context. Their new function, in Wojnarowicz's case implemented with great efficiency, was to goad those who wanted to let the epidemic take its course as a series of divine judgements on homosexuality in general.

Even within parts of the homosexual community, however, homosexual erotica came to be frowned upon, as an incitement to unsafe sexual behaviour. Meanwhile another part of the same community defended it, as a substitute for activities which were no longer prudent.

Analysing the current reception given to homosexual images and texts in the English-speaking world is a good way of examining both its deep social and ethical divisions concerning the reception of erotica in general, and also the unconscious but powerful impulse to create an *ad hoc* hierarchy of what is and is not acceptable: effectively an unspoken social and legal compromise whose terms have a tendency to vary constantly and sometimes bewilderingly.

In the United States, where material of this sort receives powerful protection from the constitution, there is much more apparent liberty than there is in Britain, but also a degree of ghettoization. Homosexual images and books are freely available in many, but not all,

ABOVE: *Page/Johnson/Johnson by* **George Duzeau**, *a classical composition that alludes to the traditional grouping of the Three Graces and celebrates the eroticism inherent in line and curve, solid and void.*

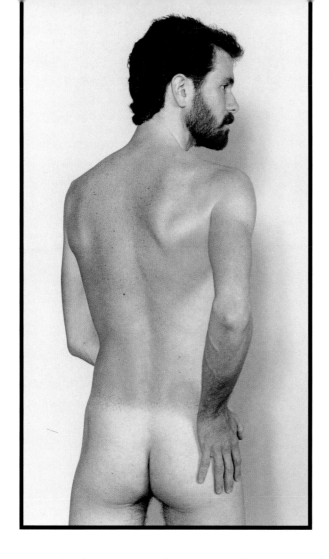

'The right lover came in the end, over the wall between the two cubicles in the cottage at the top of the hill, and lowered himself lithe and hairless (shirtless too) into David's realm. He smiled as he looked David straight in the eyes. And without a word he took David's head between his hands and kissed him. He pushed his tongue between David's lips and past his teeth, and suddenly David's mouth was open wide and full of swirling soft, non-stop tongue. He leaned back against the wall and the man leaned towards him, pushing his way further into David's mouth as he swooned unstruggling in the sweet pleasure. They didn't stop kissing, it seemed, until both had come and the queue of irritated men leaning against the stained tiles reached almost out of the door. The strange hairless man climbed over the wall again and disappeared.'

OSCAR MOORE
A MATTER OF LIFE AND SEX 1991

LEFT: *Eric, from the* Bear Cult *series by* **Chris Nelson***, presents a slim, smooth back, and an unthreatening, inviting pose.*

geographical regions of America, but largely through specialist outlets. In Britain, the division between mainstream and minority is not nearly so precise, and hard-core homosexual texts, in particular, are available in bookstores which hesitate to offer the heterosexual equivalent.

Print is considered less inflammatory than visual images. Paintings and drawings are considered less inflammatory than photographs. Erotic images in relatively expensive hardcover books are less likely to be censored than those which are available in paperbacks, and these in turn are less vulnerable than those in magazines. Videos cause far more concern than anything printed. Underlying all of this is a complex of inherited elitist attitudes about education and class. There is in addition a real sense of threat – does what is shown directly encourage imitative behaviour, or must the propensity already be present? If it is present, will repressing the images related to this behaviour suppress

the inclination itself? These questions apply to all forms of erotica but have particular force when asked in relation to material which expresses the attraction of the male for the male, since this for such a long period of time was consigned to the very deepest level of suppression.

The debate is given added force by the dawn of the digital age. Any detailed analysis of the Internet and its contents seems to demonstrate three things. Firstly, that there is a much greater appetite for erotic materials of all kinds than anyone had previously estimated. Secondly, it shows that the proportion of homosexual material on the Internet is extraordinarily high, in relation to this great mass of available text and imagery. Thirdly, it is evident that the proliferation of digital material is almost impossible to control. Inability to control one major source of information has profound implications for the status of all the rest.

RIGHT: *There was a trend in sixteenth-century France for images of women bathing together. In this painting, by a member of the School of Fontainebleau, the woman on the left, pinching her companion's finger, may be Gabrielle d'Estrees, mistress of Henry VI .*

# Women IN LOVE

*V*eactions to lesbianism have not, *traditionally, been precisely the same as reactions to male homosexuality. Where, for example, public opinion has often been ready to draw sexual inferences from close relationships between two* men, it has been much less ready to do so when the bond was between females. In the past it was much easier for two women to be lifelong companions, and live under the same roof, than it was for men who chose to behave in the same fashion. In fact, when two spinsters of a certain age chose to set up house together, it was usually considered an eminently respectable thing to do. It was far more scandalous for a woman to insist on living entirely alone.

Openly lesbian relationships were, in addition, a traditional source of erotic fascination to heterosexual males, and this fascination expressed itself frequently in art. Lesbian images seem to have combined several functions – they attempted, first, to satisfy a prurient male curiosity about what women do when they are alone together, supposedly hidden from the masculine gaze. That is, these images express feelings about the intractable 'otherness' of the opposite gender.

Secondly, Freudian theory inclines to the hypothesis that a voyeuristic interest in lesbianism is directly related to the voyeur's own castration fear. A woman who acts as if she already possessed a penis is, for the watcher, a

*'Far from the loud laughter of men, our secret life stirred.'*

CAROL ANN DUFFY *born 1955*
OPPENHEIM'S CUP AND SAUCER 1985

reassuring spectacle, since she is less likely to try and rob him of his own.

One can perhaps add a further twist to this. Male voyeurs regard lesbian activity as reassuring because it demonstrates, through its apparent incompleteness, the superiority of the masculine.

Lesbian literature and lesbian art have pursued rather different paths since antiquity. Lesbian literature is almost wholly the product of women. Sappho (c.612–580 BC), the most celebrated female poet of ancient times, gave her name, or alternatively that of her native island, Lesbos, to sexual relationships between women. But similar relationships appear hardly at all in either Greek or Roman art. It was only with the Renaissance that they became part of the artistic repertory, and until the present century the artists who portrayed them seem to have been entirely men, something which reflects the scarcity of female artists in general.

The approach taken by artists to scenes of lesbian enjoyment was at first largely mythological. The myth that fascinated them was that of Jupiter and Callisto, Callisto being a particularly obdurate nymph, a follower of the chaste goddess Diana, for whose sake the ruler of the gods was forced to transform himself into a female. The source is a passage in Ovid's *Metamorphoses*, one of the rare examples of a description of a supposedly lesbian encounter penned by a male author.

' The sun on high had passed its zenith, when [Callisto] entered a grove whose trees had never felt the axe. Here she took her quiver from her shoulders, unstrung her pliant bow, and lay down on the turf, resting her head on her painted quiver. When Jupiter saw her thus, tired and unprotected, he said: "Here is a secret of which my wife will know nothing; or if she does get to know of it, it will be worth her reproaches!"

Without wasting time he assumed the appearance and dress of Diana and spoke to the girl. "Dearest of my companions," he said, "where have you been hunting? On what mountain ridges?" She raised herself from the grass: "Greetings, divine mistress," she cried, "greater in my sight than Jove himself – I care not if he hears me!" Jove laughed to hear her words. Delighted to be preferred to himself, he kissed her – not with the restraint becoming to a maiden's kisses: and as she began to tell of her hunting exploits in the forest, he prevented her by his embrace, and betrayed his real self by a shameful action. So far from complying, she resisted him as far as a woman could – had Juno seen her she would have been less cruel – but how could a girl overcome a man, and who could defeat Jupiter? He had his way, and returned to the upper air.'[1]

As a result of this encounter, the unfortunate Callisto becomes pregnant. Her pregnancy is discovered and she is banished by a furious Diana from her band of virgin nymphs and then, to make things worse, turned into a she-bear by Jupiter's jealous wife Juno.

### Oppenheim's Cup and Saucer

'*Far from the loud laughter of men, our secret life stirred.*

*I remember her eyes, the slim rope of her spine.*
*This is your cup, she whispered, and this mine.*

*We drank the sweet hot liquid and talked dirty.*
*As she undressed me, her breasts were a mirror*

*and there were mirrors in the bed. She said Place*
*your legs around my neck, that's right. Yes.*'

CAROL ANN DUFFY *born 1955*

BELOW: *Sapphic love among the ruins of the Colosseum; this is an allegorical image by* **Frans Floris** *(1516–70), a Flemish painter who studied Roman and Florentine masters.*

ABOVE: *Detail from* Sexual Deviations *by* **Lisa Kokin**, *pays homage to the squeaky-clean all-American prom queen but clearly with a Sapphic subtext.*

The scene of Callisto's banishment, with many female nudes bathing, also became a favourite with painters, and it too has lesbian undertones.

The School of Fontainebleau in France was perhaps the first to produce lesbian paintings with supposedly 'real life' settings. Some of the artists connected with it evolved a new pictorial type, in which two women are shown bathing, always at half-length, with one reaching out to pinch the nipple of the other. These women generally seem to be intended as likenesses of royal mistresses, and the implication may be that, when deprived of their lord and master the king, these women of the harem had no satisfying sexual recourse but each other to pass away long languid days.

Depictions of lesbianism returned in some numbers only in the nineteenth century, and it was left to the great realist, Gustave Courbet, to paint the first full-scale, full-length lesbian scene which offers no mythological excuses for what it depicts. A number of other paintings by Courbet have similar implications, among them the so-called *Demoiselles de la Seine,* which shows two rather rumpled beauties fast asleep on a river bank, and it is evident that the subject had some kind of personal fascination for the artist, as it also did for Toulouse-Lautrec. Lautrec's numerous depictions of lesbian encounters form part of his documentation of life behind the scenes in some of the great Parisian brothels, where the artist sometimes took up residence for months at a time. Himself deformed (he once described himself as 'a little teapot with a big spout'), Lautrec may subconsciously have read the open lesbianism of many of the prostitutes in the *maison closes* as an egalitarian rejection of all men, not merely himself.

In the twentieth century, with a gradual increase in the number of professional artists who were women, lesbianism took on a further lease of life in art. There are paintings and drawings with homosexual connotations by a variety of female artists, among them Marie Laurencin, Jeanne Mammen, Tamara de Lempicka and the British Art Deco painter Gluck. Lempicka, though

1. *The Metamorphoses of Ovid*, translated and with an introduction by Mary M. Innes (Penguin Books, London, 1995) p. 61.

*121*

ABOVE: **Picasso** was very adept at reworking traditional themes. In 1971 he created a stunning new version of lesbians lying on a bed together. Unlike Courbet's blissed-out, exhausted lesbians, those in Femmes Nues à la Fleur have a new vitality.

twice married, was bisexual, and Laurencin may also have experimented with lesbianism. Gluck was openly homosexual. At the same time, however, male painters continued to make use of the theme, both for its intrinsic erotic impact and as a way of proclaiming their own contempt for social conventions.

The period immediately following World War I saw lesbianism become fashionable in a way that it had never been previously. The *garçonne*, or boy-girl, was recognized as a new type, and was celebrated in literature, in painting (there is a depiction of a typical *garçonne* by Kees Van Dongen, dating from c. 1923, where the subject wears an adaptation of male evening dress) and in the theatre. Her apotheosis is perhaps to be found in the Diaghilev ballet *Les Biches* of the mid-1920s, an almost entirely homosexual creation, with music by Poulenc and choreography by Bronislava Nijinska, sister of the great dancer Vaslav Nijinsky. In Paris and Berlin, women whose clothes and demeanour defiantly proclaimed their sexual inversion found an easier acceptance than had ever been available previously. Otto Dix's (1891–1969) incisively characterized portrait of the homosexual Berlin journalist Sylvia von Harden memorializes a moment of cultural history.

The rise of the dictatorships in the 1930s, with their emphasis on women as breeders and mothers, tended to drive lesbianism underground once again. In Britain, never in the forefront of sexual toleration, especially in the first half of the century, the limits had already been stated by the prosecution of Radclyffe Hall's lesbian novel *The Well of Loneliness* (1928) inspite of the fact that there is no law in the UK proscribing it. Since perceptions of the exact nuances to be found in female relationships had by then been greatly sharpened by Freud, lesbianism was for a while almost as much persecuted as male homosexuality, in spite of its extra-legal status. Its re-emergence dates from the 1970s and 1980s. Two factors seem to have been at work. One was the rise of feminism, the other the appearance of AIDS.

ABOVE: **Gerda Wegener's** illustration for The Pleasures of Eros, 1917, shows a transition in style from Art Nouveau to Art Deco. The Crinoline provides a striking contrast to that of social-realist contemporary artists such as George Grosz.

The feminist movement has never been a unity, but from the end of the 1960s it did contain within itself a strong element of lesbian separatism. It is sometimes a little difficult to decide whether the more militant separatists adopted lesbianism for political reasons, as a way of expressing disgust with a male-dominated world of social relationships, or whether separatism was a direct expression of lesbian feeling, and in a certain sense a justification of it. But the situation is even more complicated than this formulation suggests. Within feminism, women found ways of building relationships with members of their own gender which had not previously been available to them, and sometimes discovered, perhaps to their surprise, that these new relationships contained an unmistakable current of sexual feeling, which might be present without necessarily being predominant. As some of Sappho's poems indicate, lesbianism seems very often to be an available alternative,

ABOVE: **Edgar Degas'** monotype, Femmes Nues, c. 1879, is from a series of brothel scenes. These compositions anticipate similar subjects depicted by Henri de Toulouse-Lautrec who, like Degas, referred to the prevailing lesbianism in the so-called 'maisons closes'.

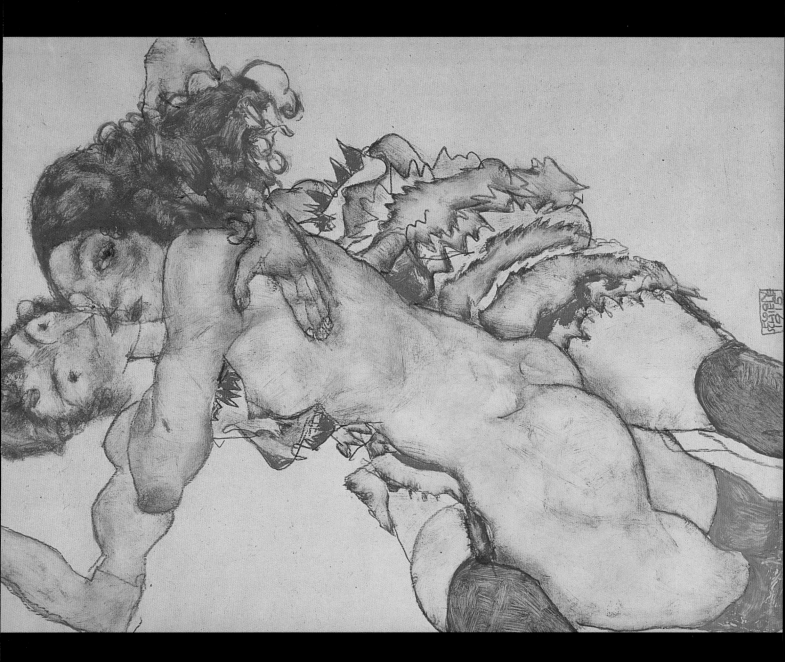

ABOVE: Produced during
World War I, Two Girls
Embracing, 1915, is one of
**Egon Schiele's** most
ambitious drawings. Less
realistic in style than much
of his work, this anticipates
Art Deco.

ABOVE: *Probably the most famous depiction of lesbianism in Western art is* **Gustave Courbet's** *1877 painting* Le Sommeil, *commissioned by an Egyptian client resident in Paris. Significantly it was executed by a rampant heterosexual for a man of the same sexual orientation.*

rather than something which demands a clear-cut choice. The same may be true of male homosexuality, but surely to a much lesser extent.

The AIDS epidemic, by removing from the scene many of the leaders of the male homosexual community, increasingly offered power within that community to lesbians. This was especially important in the United States, where homosexual separatism remained much more of an issue than it had ever become in Europe.

' I would note that at the heart of most of our issues is the realization that (at least in the USA) we, as Gay men, deviate from the cultural norms and most of us have no intention of trying to "fix" that. Indeed, most of us don't see a problem to fix...Gay men and lesbians and indeed persons of color and anything else that challenges the Ward-n-June image of reality presented by every institution in our culture are, at heart, *de facto* cultural revolutionaries. Each in our own way, as Bobby Sands said, "has his or her own part to play". '

This statement, taken from an Internet mailing list, was written by a homosexual male, but I think expresses the attitudes of a large part of the American homosexual community.

One result of these changes has been the appearance, primarily in the United States and Canada, but also increasingly often elsewhere in the English-speaking world, of an erotic literature written by females for females. This, I believe, is an entirely new phenomenon and its effects have yet to be assessed. Some of this literary output is heterosexual in orientation, but a great deal of it is either candidly lesbian, or at the very least flirts with lesbian feelings. This literature has a much more substantial public presence than either heterosexual or male homosexual equivalents, since it can offer justifications for itself that are rooted in feminist doctrine, which asserts than women have a moral right to explore their own sexual feelings – perhaps, indeed, a duty as well as a right. This may be the first occasion in the history of Western culture when eroticism has attempted to take over the high ground of morality.

Living as I do in Britain, a country which has long specialized in ambiguity where the treatment of sexual issues is concerned, it is amusing and interesting to see that, while heterosexual pornography of the Victorian epoch is now freely available and while hard-core homosexual erotica finds a place in many upmarket general bookstores, the place to look for collections of recent lesbian material of the same type has proved to be the public library.

' *And your charming laugh that honestly Makes my heart reel inside my breast For when I briefly glance at you Then speech becomes impossible.* '

SAPPHO, IX *c.612–580 BC*
TRS. TERENCE DuQUESNE

'*They slipped into a different level. Visual detail was submerged in a physical drowning, an indistinct pool of sensation. Eleanor trailed her finger across Selma's vulva, rubbing the nub of flesh above it, the harder hair, pushing her legs open, and then disappearing inside her, molten, wet, the glory of it, the beauty of that wet moving space, ribbed like the roof of a cat's mouth, bending and caressing, and Selma moaning high and not like herself by Eleanor's ear.*'

JOANNA BRISCOE *born 1963*
MOTHERS AND OTHER LOVERS 1994

BELOW: *Lesbianism has a long history of representation in Japanese art. In this late* shunga *scroll, dated c. 1870, a lesbian orgy takes place by the side of an ornamental pool.*

'It was flower into flower, breasts making love rubbing against breasts. Diana of Ephesus. '

MARGE PIERCY *born 1937*
THE HIGH COST OF LIVING 1978

ABOVE: **François Boucher** *gently hints at sapphic affections in* Les Charmantes Villageoises.

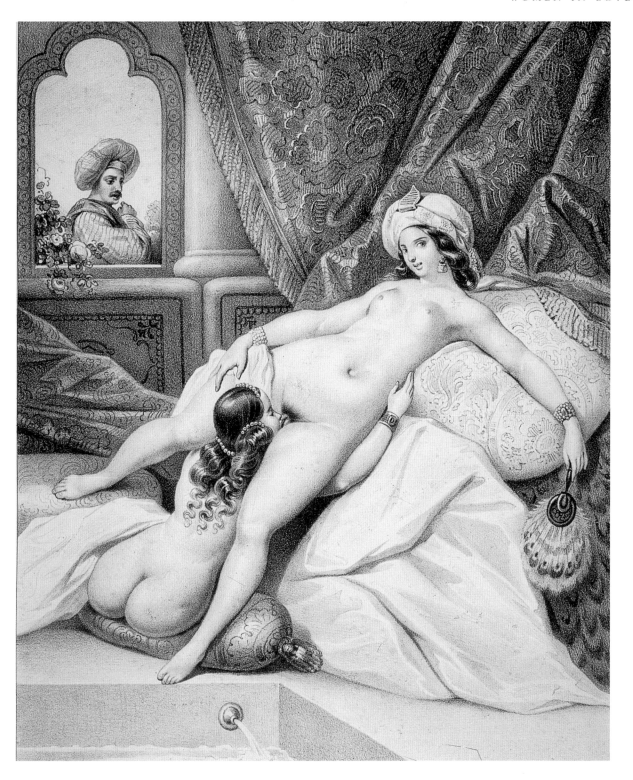

ABOVE: **Eugène Deveria's**
(1808–65) The Harem
takes to extremes the
popular oriental theme of
the first half of the
nineteenth century. Such
orientalism surpasses that
seen in Ingres' Odalisque.

129

RIGHT: The Bathers *by* **Jules Scalbert** *(1851–1901) exemplifies what was considered appropriate in French Salon painting of the late nineteenth century. The women divesting themselves are particularly forthright for the time, indicating no mythological context.*

# *En plein* AIR

S*ex in the open air* has two connotations, somewhat at variance with one another. It implies closeness to nature, sex as a ritual act of oneness with the forces which lie at the very roots of all life. It is in this sense, perhaps, that some of the greatest mythological love-paintings are to be interpreted. The pagan gods are, after all, simply the forces of nature herself, differentiated, allegorized and personified. When they make love to one another all nature responds.

There is a similar message to be learnt from the representations of nymphs and shepherds dallying with one another. These hedonistic and innocent beings, who are the natural world personified, conspicuously inhabit Western literature as well as Western art. The general assumption is that their activities represent the simplest, healthiest, least complicated form of sexual activity; that their couplings are events to which the word 'innocent' can legitimately, though perhaps somewhat paradoxically, be applied. The same sentiment applies to literature as well as to art. After all what could be jollier than this sort of thing. An anonymous seventeenth-century poem which probably began its career as a street singer's ballad, before being gathered up into some of the anthologies of erotic verse which were popular at the time, begins:

*'A man and a young maid that loved a long time*
*Were ta'en in a frenzy i' the midsummer prime.*
*The maid she lay drooping, hye,*
*The man he lay whopping, hey, the man lay whopping, ho.'*

And so on for half-a-dozen or so stanzas until the appropriate conclusion is reached:

*'The trees and the woods did wring about*
*And every leaf began to shout,*
*And there was such whopping, hye,*
*And there was such whopping, hey, there was such whopping, ho.'*

Yet not all pastoral poems are like this, or even most of them. The majority are the work of very sophisticated writers indeed. The pastoral convention which Elizabethan and Stuart poets employed so frequently is a learned one which derives from Greek writers. A reader educated in the classics, and aware of this background, must have found something deliciously daring in the opening lines of one of the reprobate Earl of Rochester's more forthright lyrics:

*'Fair Chloris in a Pig-Sty lay,*
*Her tender Herd lay by her,*
*She slept in murmuring Gruntlings, they*
*Complaining of the scorching Day,*
*Her Slumbers thus inspire.'*

But Rochester was also capable of using the convention in its more usual form:

*'As Chloris full of harmless Thoughts*
*Beneath a Willow lay,*
*Kind Love a youthful Shepherd brought*
*To pass the Time away.'*

*'From the flowers*
*A beautifully luxuriant bed...'*

WALTER VON DER VOGELWEIDE
*c. 1170–1230*
UNDER THE LINDEN

ABOVE: *Parisian society was outraged by* **Edouard Manet's** Déjeuner sur l'herbe *of 1863 due to its grouping of contemporarily clothed men with nude female figures.*

These literary conventions, or hopes, inevitably have an air of condescension about them. Most pastoral poetry was almost by definition written by people who were far from living the pastoral life themselves, and the only innocence it possesses is mock innocence. Perhaps the most refined expression of this mock-rural sensibility, at least in terms of the visual arts, is the eighteenth-century *fête champêtre*, as painted by Watteau and his slightly more daring disciple Pater (1695–1736). Here elegant company disports itself on the very verge of sexual indiscretion, but almost never crosses the line.

For a more realistic view of outdoor sex we have to turn to prose writers rather than poets. One of those is the author of *My Secret Life*. Here he is in his youth, having sexual congress with a servant girl:

' The more she objected, the more
I longed for her. At last under solemn promise that I would go away after, we turned up a short street leading into a lane by garden-grounds, and there up against a fence I fucked her. Away she went, and I never saw her afterwards to speak to, though I have passed her without taking notice. I think that in that parting fuck I had all the pleasure, she none. '[1]

And here he is with a woman hay-maker:

' As I left the farm-gate, female hay-makers who had worked till dark passed, curtseying as they recognised me. I thought of Whiteteeth [a woman he had already noticed] but saw her not. Turning back from Pender's after I had strolled past the cottage, I went up the lane languishing with lust, and leaned against a field-gate. I heard a step – it was the woman with the white teeth.
   "Good night." "Good night, sir." "Come here." She stopped, came close. I laid hold of her arm and drew her close to the gate. "Come into the field with me. I will give you five shillings."
   A slight chuckle, the white teeth show. "I dare not." But as she spoke I had her back up against the gate, my hand on her grummit.
   "My old man will be waiting for me, – I can't." Lifting her clothes I tried to impale her as she stood. "No, no, – someone will pass," said she in a whisper. I put my hand on the latch, the gate opened, and we were in the field; the gate closed with a snap. I led her along by a ditch to a turn in the hedge; she made no resistance, in a minute we were buried in deep grass, my doodle buried in her cunt, we had spoken in whispers, all was silent except for the insects which chirped in the hot summer night. '[2]

The vivid directness and particularity of Walter's descriptions of sexual activity are hard to match in art of the same period – the second half of the nineteenth century. The painting which most successfully tested the boundaries of discretion, and made its author notorious in the process of doing so, is Manet's *Déjeuner sur l'herbe*. What precisely does the painting show, and why did it cause such an uproar? The Emperor Napoleon III, himself no paragon of sexual morality, was so affronted by it that he is said to have struck it with his whip when he was confronted by it in the Salon des Refusés.

The composition, as is generally known, was not original to Manet (1832–83), but derives from an engraving by Marcantonio Raimondi (the engraver of Giulio Romano's *I Modi*) after a composition by Raphael. This composition is a generic mythological scene, showing nude figures in the open air. The engraving itself circulated widely in the studios of Manet's time.

Manet's offence was to put two of the four figures into contemporary dress. His two males are fully clothed, and wear the kind of costume worn by students and aspiring artists. The implication is that these are two young painters who have taken their models, who are also pretty certainly their mistresses, to some rural location and persuaded them to undress. They are now idly enjoying this immodest display. The fact that the men remain clothed, and wear what was then contemporary dress, made, and indeed still makes, the women seem even more naked than they might if they did not have these companions. There was no fuss, for

'*She lay down there under the boughs while he waited, standing there in his shirt and breeches, watching her with haunted eyes* '

D. H. LAWRENCE *1885–1930*
LADY CHATTERLEY'S LOVER 1928

1. Walter, *My Secret Life I*, Vols 1, 2, 3 & 4 (Arrow Books, London, 1984) p. 549.
2. op. cit. p. 227.

ABOVE: *In this scene from a nineteenth-century Chinese 'pillow book', the outdoor setting has been rigorously formalized. It is interesting to note the bound feet of the girl.*

example, about the large paintings showing nymphs bathing which Manet's older contemporary Corot (1796–1875) was producing at about the same period, even though the individual nudes are quite as realistically depicted as those shown by Manet. However, no member of the opposite sex is present, and this, in terms of the time, excused everything.

Manet's painting offended in another, subtler way as well. Two familiar formulae in European art for showing nudes of the opposite sex together *en plein air* was to make the work either a representation of the so-called 'Golden Age', a mythical epoch when both the idea of sin and the need for clothing were alike unknown, or else a representation of the Fall. Lucas Cranach the Elder did a number of Golden Age paintings featuring a multiplicity of nudes: males and females, adults and

ABOVE: *Diana discovering the Pregnancy of Callisto, a favourite and much painted mythological scene and splendid excuse to show a multitude of nude female figures in the open air. This version is by* Jan van Neck *(1635–1714), a Dutch Italianate painter.*

'*He came closer to her. She let him.*'

ANAÏS NIN 1903–77
THE WOMAN ON THE DUNES

ABOVE; *A perverse medical examination of a blindfolded, tattooed woman takes place in* **Wei Dong's** *1995 anachronistic picture* Early Qing Landscape – Performance.

*The scene is seemingly set in the seventeenth century, when the stethoscope was not yet invented and Mao's* Little Red Book, *being read by the figure on the left, certainly did not exist.*

'*He tried to imagine her naked, shutting his eyes against the dappled canopy above him, altering his position to allow his swelling erection a chance to shift freely beneath his trousers. A wand of sunlight beamed through a gap in the leaves above him and warmed his flank. Holding these images in his mind, embellishing them, he reached for his handkerchief with one hand while his other tremblingly undid the buttons of his fly.* '

WILLIAM BOYD *born 1952*
THE BLUE AFTERNOON 1993

children, for the Saxon court. The Fall, however, was a much more popular subject. For many artists it became a way of having their cake and eating it, of displaying their command of the nude and at the same time paying appropriate tribute to the Judaeo-Christian condemnation of nudity. In Dürer's (1471–1528) famous engraving of Adam and Eve (1504), as in so many other versions of the same subject, the ancestors of the human race are 'clothed' with the leaves which are the emblems of their transgression against God's command. In Manet's painting, the atmosphere is flatly secular.

It is of course amusing to reflect that only the world-wide celebrity of the painting protects it against similar reactions today. It is hard to think of any masterpiece in the whole established canon of Western art which is less in tune with the whole doctrine of political correctness. His clothed males, in modern feminist terms, are clearly phallocratic oppressors of their nude companions, and invite any male spectator to react in the same manner.

Yet there is perhaps more to it than this. Sex which does not take place in an enclosed or hidden space, which is not under a roof is by definition not in any way ashamed of itself. It takes place 'under the eye of heaven' and by implication takes into account the possibility of other observers as well. The urgency of the impulse, so the setting itself implies, disregards all social restraints. Passion links hands with opportunism. One of the peculiarities of sexual representations in art (though not necessarily of sexual acts described in words) is that it always implies the presence of an observer, and often insists that such an observer is present. In this sense, the natural setting, the innocence which it implies, are always a sham. The serpent is already present in Eden, the possibility of shame exists even in the images where it is most strenuously denied.

ABOVE: *This 1930 work of the influential teacher* **André Lhote** *(1885–1962) entitled Leda, is a modern take on this enduring myth. It also exemplifies inter-war sun worship and subsequent enthusiasm for the Mediterranean.*

## Under the Linden

'Under the linden
Near the common
Where both of us had shared a bed;
There, lying where we'd lain,
You'll come upon
Some grass and flowers neatly spread.
Outside the forest in the dell
tarantara!
sweetly sang the nightingale.

I came there only
To discover
My darling was already there;
That was when he called me
'Divine Creature':
I'll always hold that greeting dear.
Some kisses! More than ten hundred!
tarantara!
that's what made my lips so red.

I saw he'd made us
From the flowers
A beautifully luxuriant bed;
Some stranger who might pass
This bed of ours
Will smile, knowing why it was made.
The roses give the game away,
tarantara!
they reveal where my head lay.

If anyone knew
He'd slept with me
(Which God forbid!) I'd die of shame;
What our bodies did and how
No one will know
Except, that is, for me and him
And of course the little bird,
tarantara!
who's not going to say a word.'

WALTER VON DER VOGELWEIDE
c. 1170–1230

BELOW: *Untitled by* **Timothy Cummings** *(b. 1968) looks back to fourteenth-century manuscript illustration in its bright jewel colours and the literary convention of courtly love; the walled secret garden (hortus conclusus) was a favourite obliquely erotic image.*

' *Thus talking and walking they came to a place...* '

ANON
A MAN AND A YOUNG MAID

ABOVE: *Watteau's close disciple,* **Jean-Baptiste Joseph Pater** *here extends the theme of the* fête champêtre *to* show a Bathing Party in a Park. *The emphasis on the central figure's buttocks is typical of the period.*

'*If the forest of her hair*
*calls you to explore the land,*
*And her breasts, those mountains fair,*
*Tempt that mountaineer, your hand –*
*Stop! before it is too late:*
*Love, the brigand, lies in wait.*'

BHARTRHABI *5th century*
TRS. JOHN BROUGH

ABOVE: A Couple Making Love Whilst Riding a Camel, *painted in Rajasthan in 1790, is a delightfully perverse image from one of the most romantic of the Rajput schools of painting, the* **Bundi-Khota***.*

BELOW: *A Chinese scroll painting of around 1850 shows an invading Mongol horsemen himself being pleasurably mounted. There is a pun in the Chinese language: 'to mount' means 'to fuck'.*

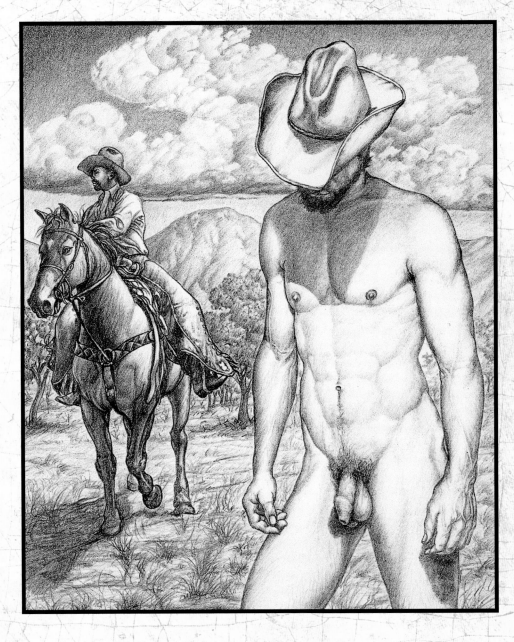

ABOVE: *American artist,* **Delmas Howe***, combines classical and Western themes in his 1996 lithograph Hermes. The nudity of Hermes, the god of travellers, implies that he stalks through the night invisible to the cowboy riding in close proximity.*

## A Man and a Young Maid

*A man and a young maid that loved a long time*
*Were ta'en in a frenzy i' the midsummer*
*prime.*
*The maid she lay drooping, hye,*
*The man he lay whopping, hey, the man lay*
*whopping, ho.*

*Thus talking and walking they came to a place*
*Environed about with trees and with grass*
*The maid she, etc.*

*He shifted his hand whereas he had placed;*
*He handled her knees instead of her waist.*
*The maid, etc.*

*He shifted his hand till he came to her knees.*
*He tickled her and she opened her thighs,*
*Yet still she, etc.*

*He hottered and tottered, and there was a lane*
*That drew him on forward. He went on*
*amain,*
*Yet still she, etc.*

*The lane it was strait; he had not gone far,*
*He lit in a hole ere he was aware.*
*But she fell a-kissing, hye,*
*And he lay drooping, ho, and he lay drooping,*
*ho.*

*"My Billy, my pilly! How now?" quoth she.*
*"Get up again, Billy, if that thou lovest me".*
*Yet still he lay, etc.*

*He thought mickle shame to lie so long.*
*He got up again and grew very strong.*
*The maid she lay, etc.*

*The trees and the woods did wring about*
*And every leaf began to shout,*
*And there was such whopping, hye,*
*And there was such whopping, hey, there was*
*such whopping, ho.* '

A N O N

ABOVE: *Arethusa the wood nymph pursued by the river god Alpheius who fell in love with her. Dutch seventeenth-century painter,* **Moyses van Uyttenbroeck**, *(c.1595–1648) transforms the myth into an earthy peasant scene in this 1626 painting, Alphée poursuivant Arethuse.*

BELOW: **Masami Teraoka's** Kunisada Eclipsed, 1995, *painted in the Hokusai style but reversing the scales, making* the people huge and the waves tiny; the girl's buttocks outshine anything the sea or sky can produce.

ABOVE: *This composition,*
*entitled* The Bathers
*(c.1765), shows the Rococo*
*master* **Fragonard** *at his*
*most exuberant. Female flesh*
*is transmuted into freely*
*brushed paint.*

' *She continued to swim,*
*and he repeated his passage over her. Then she stood up,*
*and he drove down and passed between her legs.*
*They laughed. They both moved with*
*ease in the water.*

*He was deeply excited. He swam with his sex hard.*
*Then they approached each other*
*with a crouching motion, as if for a battle.*
*He brought her body against his, and she*
*felt the tautness of his penis.* '

ANAÏS NIN *1903–77*
THE WOMAN ON THE DUNES

# *Solitary* PLEASURES

RIGHT: **Jean Rustin** is one of the most disturbing contemporary artists. In his 1988 painting I am Not Happy Here, *from a series on* the same theme, he has turned female masturbation into a savagely aggressive act, a sign of distress and disorientation.

*n*ot surprisingly, perhaps, solitary sexual pleasures have left the fewest traces in either art or literature. The paradox is, of course, that both erotic texts and erotic representations often owe their existence to the fact that they provide material for masturbatory fantasy. Masturbation is regarded, first as juvenile – as the occupation of those who are only just discovering their sexuality and who have not yet mastered the business of getting partners for themselves; secondly, it is thought of as a last resort, a release for those who for whatever reason cannot get partners at all.

Where juvenile masturbation was concerned, the nineteenth-century medical profession was obsessed by the subject. It was thought to weaken the practitioner by draining away some form of vital spinal fluid. In order to combat it, all sorts of ingenious 'chastity' devices were invented. Into these the unfortunate juvenile was confined. One, meant for adolescent boys, generated an electrical charge and rang a bell to wake the wearer whenever he got an involuntary erection.

This obsession is of course linked to the general nineteenth-century obsession with sexuality. We should, however, be careful in our evaluation of this. Obsessive fear of sex, and disapproval of nearly all forms of sexual activity, arrived much later on the scene, and lasted for a shorter period than is usually estimated. The early Victorians took more robust attitudes towards sex than is usually realized today. Many, especially amongst the aristocracy, retained the relaxed sexual attitudes of the reign of George IV. A case in point was Lord Palmerston, one of Victoria's most successful prime ministers, and notorious for his mistresses. Palmerston's aristocratic background, which in turn governed the type of upbringing he received, was of course an important factor. When we talk of 'Victorian' attitudes to sex we often speak as if these were prevalent from top to bottom of society. This was clearly not the case. Aristocrats, with admittedly some exceptions, tended to regard these restrictions as rules which applied to people other than themselves. The vast mass of the working poor also had little time or energy to think of such matters, as can be seen from Henry Mayhew's vast compendium on *The Life and Labour of the London Poor* (4 vols, 1851–62).

One reason why we now tend to over-estimate even late Victorian repressiveness is that our access to the attitudes of the time is now almost entirely through the printed page, and here sexual issues did undoubtedly

*'Dildoes – they come in varied size and shape – five foot, five six, six foot, fair, middling, dark.'*

FIONA PITT-KETHLEY *born 1954*
DILDOES

'*I have masturbated so much that by now I am madly in love with myself. I am a young woman, beautiful, I have longings and desires…*'

TERESINKA PEREIRA *born 1940*
NARCISSUS WOMAN

BELOW: *One of the striking things about* **Schiele's** *art is his power to transform brutally frank depictions of* sexuality, such as Girl Masturbating, *into images of superb draughtsmanship and high aesthetic quality.*

create a great deal of noise. Even here, however, we must be careful in the judgements we make. At the very height of the most repressive period in Britain, the newspapers, in particular *The Times*, the bible of the English establishment, printed full details of the most scandalous divorce cases of the time. The right of newspapers to report this kind of material was only to be restrained much later, in the 1920s. Such material must have provided rich stimulation on occasion for masturbatory fantasy. Why resort to fiction, when factual reporting had as much, or even more to offer in the way of sexual stimulus for the solitary hedonist?

What we do find, towards the end of the century, is the growth of a new set of attitudes, where repression is

questioned and yet in a certain sense both reinforced and celebrated. The rebellion began, perhaps surprisingly, in Britain. It manifests itself in certain aspects of late Pre-Raphaelitism, and perhaps most obviously in the Pre-Raphaelite cult of the fatal woman. The linkage of sexual love and death is carried still further in the work of an important poet who is now perhaps the most neglected figure in the whole of nineteenth-century literature in English. The publication of Algernon Charles Swinburne's *Poems and Ballads: First Series* in 1866 marks the moment when the tide first began to turn against middle-class repression.

There is another and even more cogent reason for citing Swinburne at this point which is that, as has long

ABOVE: *Solipsism and security; in* **Arthur Tress's** *1980 photograph, the subject lies in a cosy cocoon, abandoned to pleasure, apparently vulnerable but somehow insulated in his own world, untroubled by the lowering city behind him; the two worlds simply do not touch.*

been recognized, his most typical literary productions are essentially outpourings of masturbatory fantasy. His once notorious poem *Dolores*, with its obsessive rhythm and sado-masochistic imagery, is as perfect a reflection as can be imagined of a certain sort of sexual reverie:

> ' *O lips full of lust and of laughter,*
> *Curled snakes that are fed from my breast,*
> *Bite hard, lest remembrance come after*
> *And press with new lips where you pressed,*
> *For my heart too springs up at the pressure,*
> *Mine eyelids too moisten and burn;*
> *Ah, feed me and fill me with pleasure,*
> *Ere pain come in turn.* '

One may reasonably suspect that one of the things which most disturbed Swinburne's critics was the fact that nothing very specifically sexual is described. It is the rhythm, and the descriptions of an imaginary dominatrix in her savage glory, which give the poem its force.

Representations of the actual act of masturbation have to be looked at in a different way from descriptions of, and incitements to, masturbatory activity in literary texts. The author of *My Secret Life* is a good guide here, as in so many other matters to do with sexuality. Walter has a certain distaste for the act of 'frigging', as he calls it. As a means of release, it is very much a thing of last resort. Later, as he grows older, and his sexual tastes become more complicated, he develops a liking, only very occasionally indulged however, for handling the private parts of other males. But these pleasures, obviously, are not 'solitary'.

In the eighteenth century, makers of galant images – Boucher and his followers in France, Rowlandson (1756–1827) in Britain – sometimes offer images of females (never males, as far as I am aware) masturbating. Their purpose is of course provocative. The female has had to resort to this because she is in urgent need of a man, a need which the viewer may imagine himself as supplying. In its most daring form, female masturbation is placed in an exhibitionistic context.

In one Rowlandson print, for example, a woman masturbates on a platform, before a circle of gawping,

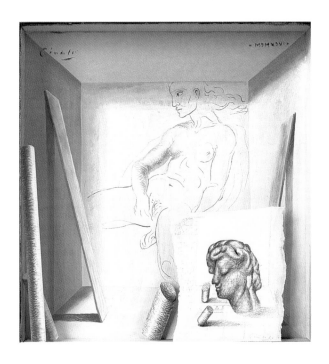

ABOVE: *Here self-stimulation becomes a theatrical act. The* mise-en scene *is created by the young Argentinian artist*  **Ricardo Cinalli**, *who specializes in painted boxes with images presented as if they are appearing on stage.*

' *A wank is always liable to be slightly disappointing if what you really want is a fuck; but if what you really want is a wank, you can't beat it.* '

MARTIN AMIS

lecherous men. Her power over them, the design implies, is absolute. Far from being exploited, she is the one who exploits her slavering audience.

The situation only begins to change at the very beginning of the present century. Some of the most graphic representations of female masturbation ever produced in a Western context (equally graphic ones are sometimes found, however, in Japanese *shunga*) are the work of the Austrian artist Egon Schiele (1890–1918). Schiele, a superb draughtsman, unmatched in the twentieth century by any artist (save the much longer lived and therefore far more prolific Picasso) made something of a speciality of images of women stimulating themselves. His models are often very young girls, which makes his representations of them the more provocative. Not content with this, Schiele also drew a number of self-portraits in which he himself is masturbating. If we discount a few images of Greek satyrs on vases, these are the first really candid representations of the act in Western art.

Schiele came from a very special society, the Vienna which also nurtured Freud. It is clear from his art that he saw himself as the living embodiment of the neurasthenia which Freud was the first to examine in scientific or would-be scientific terms. The modes of behaviour in his drawings were things to celebrate, because they showed the utmost contempt for bourgeois propriety.

I can think of only one other artist who has stressed female masturbation to the same extent that Schiele did, and this is the contemporary French artist Jean Rustin (born 1926). Rustin's story is as strange as that of his Viennese predecessor. Trained at the Ecole des Beaux-Arts in Paris, he became a well-respected French abstract painter, who achieved a major retrospective exhibition at

ABOVE: **François Boucher's** Girl Urinating *has a similar atmosphere to erotic novels of the* same period, combining realism and squalor with elegance, the swish of silk and the hot reek of urine.

### Signior Dildo

' You ladies all of merry England
Who have been to kiss the Duchess's hand,
Pray, did you lately observe in the show
A noble Italian called Signior Dildo?

You'll take him at first for no person of note
Because he appears in a plain leather coat
But when you his virtuous abilities know,
You'll fall down and worship Signior Dildo.

Our dainty fine duchesses have got a trick
To dote on a fool for the sake of his prick;
The fops were undone, did Their Graces but know
The discretion and vigour of Signior Dildo.

This Signior is sound, safe, ready, and dumb
As ever was candle, carrot or thumb;
Then away with these nasty devices, and show
How you rate the just merits of Signior Dildo. '

JOHN WILMOT,
2ND EARL OF ROCHESTER
1647–80

ABOVE: In Girl Raising her Skirt *(1942)*, **Boucher** reveals a fascination with the female buttocks, an obsession shared with the infamous Marquis de Sade.

155

the Musée de l'Art Moderne de la Ville de Paris in 1971.

Shortly before this, he started to turn towards figurative imagery, inspired in part by the so-called *evennements* of 1968. His retrospective showing, combined with personal traumas, inspired an almost complete revulsion against everything he had so far painted. Rustin retired into his studio, and exhibited very little for the space of ten years. During this time he remade himself as a now completely figurative painter.

Rustin's current work has sometimes been compared to that of Francis Bacon (1909–92), but is in fact much more specific in its imagery. His figures, often decrepit, confront the viewer with aggressively sexual gestures. A woman masturbating is an especially typical image. Expression and gesture make it plain that the act is a gesture of defiance and anger. Schiele's sly eroticism is here

### The Jokes of Early Aviation

*' The jokes of early aviation*
*were all about joysticks and cockpits –*

*the wartime ones, that rocked the aircrews,*
*were about pressing tits*
*and airscrews –*

*mechanical, verbal fornication,*
*and light relief for tomcat tomfools,*
*for dirty Dick and handsome Harry*
*(never, though good with tools,*
*would marry) –*

*as Mars, the god of masturbation,*
*held thousands there earthbound and grounded,*
*they praised with voices, not with bodies,*
*and seldom in a bed,*
*a Goddess. '*

GAVIN EWART *1916–1993*

# ' *The jokes of early aviation were all about joysticks and cockpits —* '

GAVIN EWART 1916–1993
THE JOKES OF EARLY AVIATION

ABOVE: *This study by* **Jean-François Gaté** *embodies the languor of long hot afternoons of self delight, oblique light slanting through a window shade, the slow, pleasurable drift of time after sex. The thing which gives this image its languidly erotic quality is not simply the pose, but the use of the wooden element supporting the chair arm as a phallic metaphor.*

ABOVE: Floating in Red,
1995. *A male figure in a*
*self-absorbed, narcissistic*
*pose by the contemporary*
*German artist* **Sara**
**Rossberg** *(b. 1952).*

transformed into a gesture of open contempt, mingled with despair at the condition of the world. Rustin's masturbating females are declarations, not so much of opposition to the current state of things, but of an all-encompassing nihilism.

Images of male masturbation have also taken on a new significance in recent years, as part of the general loosening of bonds where homosexual imagery is concerned. Before the rise of modernism, and the consequent collapse of the old academic system, images of the male nude did not necessarily possess specific sexual significance. A curious situation existed: images of the female were more likely to suggest sexual intent, but the male genitalia were thought of as being more threatening. After the time of the ancient Greeks, males were very seldom depicted in a state of erection, and when this happened, the intention was unmistakably erotic. Even on these occasions, the erect male (most usually a satyr, or half-human half-animal creature) almost invariably appeared as a component in an erotic narrative.

When photography made its appearance in the nineteenth century, male nudes were subjects for the camera as well as female ones, but at first they, much more than their female equivalents, were always presented either as the object of scientific study (as in the pioneering sequential images analysing motion made by Eadweard Muybridge and others), or else as a 'reference for artists' in standard life-class poses. At the beginning of the present century photography of the male moved towards the openly erotic in the hands of the Baron von Glöden and a few others, and photographs of this sort were quite widely circulated, though always privately.

The first significant shift came with the 'democratization' of erotic male nude photography in the very late 1950s and early 1960s. This took place largely on the West Coast of America, in the hands of commercial but still nominally 'underground' photographers such as Bob Mizer of the Athletic Model Guild and of Bruce of Los Angeles. The recent re-publication of the complete run of Athletic Model Guild catalogues by a major German publisher of art books charts the progress of permissiveness – from jockstraps and other means of concealment to frontal nudity and finally to the occasional appearance of a fully erect penis. Today most pictorial magazines addressed to a homosexual audience are quite unabashed about showing male genitalia in a state of excitation, and these publications are widely distributed and seldom fall foul of the law. Even when the model's hand is not actually on his penis, as it often is, a masturbatory situation is implied. Robert Mapplethorpe, often thought of as a pioneer in these matters, thanks to some pictures of men masturbating made in the late 1970s, was actually doing no more than keep pace with the commercial sector. Since then a number of well-known 'art' photographers, some of them female, like Nan Goldin, have incorporated into their repertoires pictures of males either masturbating or actually ejaculating. Meanwhile the progress of the AIDS epidemic has given solitary sexual activity a respectability, and indeed a discussability, which it has never known previously.

# Coming
# TOGETHER

*t*he idea of group sex has always had enormous erotic appeal, for several reasons, not just one. First, multiplicity of sexual partners suggests pleasure itself will be multiplied to the same degree. Secondly, group sex suggests an abandonment of all inhibitions, consequent upon an abandonment of shame. This second aspect offers the reason why sexual activity involving more than two people has often been repressed by law. It flouts the marriage-bond, and, more than this, it flouts the idea that sex is supposed to be a private, indeed as far as possible a completely secret activity. For the same reason, group sex is one of the staples of literary pornography. Pornography which acknowledges its own character is, through that very acknowledgement, deliberately transgressive. A large part of its appeal is that is offers readers something they believe to be forbidden. Were it not forbidden, it is very likely that a great part of its attraction would be lost.

In particular, scenes involving several partners are a regular feature of the erotic books published in Victorian times, when the rule of repressive morality was at its height. The following comes from one of the best known novels of this type, *The Adventures of Lady Harpur*, first published in 1885:

*'Now my body betrays me. It melts again, longing to be in Eve's bed with her and Frank… I just lie in my own sweat, feel my ass and my crotch join in a wide-mouthed pulsing of pleasure.'*

UNSIGNED

EAVESDROPPING 1984

' All this time, Frances was sitting on the soft carpet, while we reclined around her. Dick lay on his back in front, his hand playing with my cunt, while his prick was exulting under the stimulating touches of her cunning fingers; meanwhile I devoted my attention to his lordship's manly tool, rubbing it to my face and kissing off the pearly drop which appeared from time to time on its rosy summit. Lord Ferrars kept both his hands employed touching us all in turn, and, what I deemed a little unnatural, took especial notice of the choice qualities of my husband's fine standing prick. He grasped its firm column in his hand, and slowly pushing down the soft skin made it lift its purple head more proudly than ever.

Frances, putting her finger on it, said, "My Lord, would you not like to see this going into Queenie's cunt? It's such jolly fun to watch husband and wife fucking. They do it in such a businesslike manner. Come, dear Queenie, turn over on your back, spread your thighs and raise them as much as you can, so as to give us a full view of your beautiful bottom and all the luscious chinks there! It is a beauty! Venus Callipyge never made a more magnificent display! And see, my lord, what a cunt! So prominent! So plump, and so ripe and rosy! The view of such an enchanting slit as this, with its deep crimson folds, bathed in moisture and palpitating with desire, makes me regret I am not indeed a man, able to plunge in my prick and revel in the joy it is longing to feel and impart; but as that cannot be, I must give way to one who can. So, come here, Dick, and after my grand speech, let me arrange you according to my fancy. Now my lord, if you will pop in the prick and tickle her cunt and bottom, I will manipulate his balls and stimulate him behind. '[1]

1. Anonymous, *The Adventures of Lady Harpur* (Wordsworth Editions Limited, Ware, Hertfordshire, 1996) p. 253.

RIGHT: *First published in 1835, and reprinted in 1908, this lithograph* Rub a Dub Dub, Three in a Tub *by* **Peter Fendi** (1796–1842) *reflects the erotic world described in* My Secret Life *(1888–1892) by 'Walter'.*

FAR RIGHT: *This Rajasthani erotic miniature from the early nineteenth century depicts a prince enjoying several women. The hierarchy of the individual figures is indicated by their proportionate scale, a common technique in Indian art. The voracious prince is far larger than any of his entourage.*

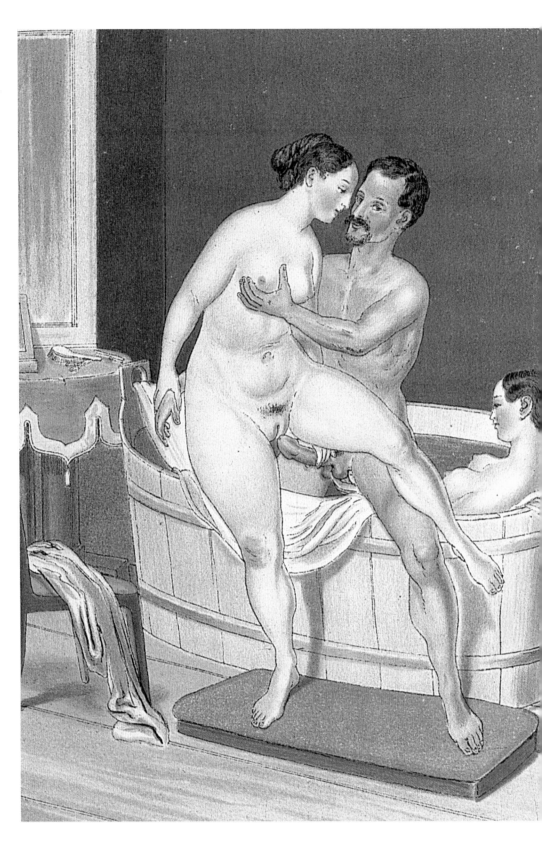

This excerpt offers a number of features typical of books of this kind. The anonymous author emphasizes the strong element of voyeurism involved in acts of group sex, and he (one assumes it was a he) also hints slyly at the possibilities offered for crossing the boundaries of heterosexuality.

Victorian erotic novels offer a number of other recurring themes. Perhaps the most interesting is the stress nearly all of them put on the shifting nature of sexual dominance. The majority of these stories, either anonymous or pseudonymous but fairly clearly written by men, are told in the first person, by a woman. A young and beautiful female is initiated sexually. Her reluctance, if she feels any, is soon overcome, and she develops an insatiable appetite for the sexual act. At first she may have some ideas of fidelity to her original lover, but she is very soon relieved of these – perhaps placed in a situation where she is forced to abandon such scruples by the lover himself. A picaresque series of adventures follows. Sometimes the intrepid heroine is placed in situations when she is forced to have sex, whether she wants to or not; at one time, for example, Lady Harpur is captured by pirates and raped, something which ruffles her composure very little. In general, however, she is an initiator and organizer: even when she appears to submit, she is in fact in control. The picture it offers of Victorian womanhood is very different from that proffered in the mainstream novels of the same epoch, where female characters are much more likely to end up as victims, and totally lack the pragmatism and sheer resilience of the women portrayed in the 'underground' fiction of the time. In Victorian pornography, sexual immorality is more often than not rewarded with material success, rather than by the disasters visited upon mainstream heroines who stray from the path of virtue.

There is, however, another kind of erotic fiction, in which multiple couplings are presented in a slightly different fashion. One might call these 'harem' stories, since the central character is always a male of inexhaustible sexual stamina, whose virility is rewarded

by the possession of a whole troupe of compliant women. Orientalism played a prominent role in both nineteenth-century art and nineteenth-century literature, and at the very centre of the fashion for things Eastern was the myth of the odalisque: the beautiful, mysterious and ever-willing female slave, always ready to place her body at the service of her master.

' ...he came close to us, and eagerly watching my prick as it darted in and out, pushed his hand in between us and felt the lips of her cunt stretched around my tool. He hardly gave me time to get off before he was on her, with his virgin prick deep in the hot recess which I had moistened and prepared for his entrance. He quickly discharged and then almost immediately commenced a second course, to Susan's intense gratification. I also shared in their fun and fingered their privates while they fucked. '

THE ADVENTURES OF LADY HARPUR 1885

In painting, slavery and the harem served as a pretext for a whole series of erotic fantasies whose candour did not prevent them from being exhibited in the official Salons of the time, often to much acclaim. One specialist in the genre was Ingres, the greatest early nineteenth-century painter of the female nude. Another artist attracted to it was Ingres' rival Delacroix. Later in the nineteenth century Jean-Léon Gerôme (1824–1904), one of the chief opponents of Impressionism, specialized in slave-market and harem scenes. The most successful of all these works, in purely financial terms, was *The Babylonian Slave Market*, painted in 1875 by the now all-but-forgotten Edwin Long (1829–91). For a long time the price paid for this was a record for a contemporary work of art.

The fantasies generated by these paintings were immune from censure because they were not written down. Erotic novels and stories which pursued the same

ABOVE: Ancient Times, *a Roman orgy imagined by the twentieth-century artist* **Edouard-Henri Avril** *(1849–1928), one of a set of illustrations that he made for* De Figuris Veneris, *an erotic work written by the mysterious F. K. Such depravities, unthinkable to respectable late Victorians, were sanctioned by the patina of antiquity.*

sort of imagery to its logical conclusion were of course necessarily clandestine. A crude but intermittently amusing example is a novella serialized in *The Pearl*, an erotic magazine which appeared between 1879 and 1880. *La Rose d'Amour*, or *The Adventures of a Gentleman in Search of Pleasure* tells the story of a wealthy young man who, having already acquired a number of women, travels to Constantinople in order to complete his harem.

164

ABOVE: *Thronging together, the Committees who stand in judgement of the Phallic Contest, vigorously represented on a Japanese* shunga *scroll.*

' *They would lie on their stomachs, still dressed, open a new book and read together, with their hands caressing each other. They kissed over erotic pictures. Their mouths, glued together, fell over enormous protruding women's asses, legs open like a compass, men squatting like dogs, with huge members almost dragging the floor.* '

ANAÏS NIN *1903–77*
ELENA

Having secured merchandise of the best quality, he returns to his château in Brittany with a group of beautiful young women who are prepared to satisfy him sexually in every way:

> ' The lovely creatures I have just been naming gathered round me, they embraced me in every part; some a leg and a thigh; others hung around my neck; some seized on my hands with which they frigged themselves; one seats herself on the floor between my legs and playfully squeezes my stones and strokes my once more rampant prick. The luscious Celeste has her arms clasped round my neck and I am about to impale her with my prick, but Fanny comes forward and urges her claim in favour of her little maidenhead, which is consuming her with a burning fever. '2

Unlike the other nineteenth-century erotic tales I have described, those which fall into this category, the harem story, usually show very few efforts at characterization: they are erotic daydreams, simple if not pure. In the example I have cited, the hero is just a penis-rampant. His partners are ciphers. The story itself has little or no incident. The collector acquires what he wishes to acquire, with a minimum of trouble. Some of his acquisitions are virgins and some are not, but none struggle very hard to retain that condition during the course of the narrative. In due course their lord and master makes use of all of them. Then he uses them again. And this is the sum total of the plot. Satiety and boredom are the result.

Paintings and other works of art, in addition to suffering less in this case from the rigours of censorship, were less apt to induce satiety. The harems of the West existed more conveniently in art, and had indeed done so long before the Romantic Movement promoted an enthusiasm for all things Eastern. The painter, and to a lesser extent the sculptor, could put as many nude bodies into conjunction as he liked, without making any kind of overt breach of the prevailing moral codes. The great mythological compositions of Western art may seldom actually show the act of coition, but the majority are sexually charged, and a great deal of that charge derives from the presence of so many naked figures, crowded together within the same pictorial space. Titian's *Diana and Her Nymphs*, despite its subject, is far from being a celebration of chastity. It is, rather, a declaration of concupiscence.

2. *The Pearl, Three Eortic Tales* (Wordsworth Editions Limited, Ware, Hertfordshire, 1985) p. 194.

ABOVE: **Wei Dong** *has
executed his modern Chinese
erotic scene,* Wishes for a
Long Life, *1966, in a
deliberately archaic style.*

‘ *…soon I was being undressed by all
three M. brothers. I can still imagine
the throbbing in my body as I felt
my clitoris swell with excitement.* ’

NANCY FRIDAY

MIA'S FANTASY FROM WOMEN ON TOP 1991

ABOVE: *Despite the mythological veneer,* **Rubens'** *hearty sexual appetite radiates from this Diana and her Nymphs* Surprised by Fauns. *Surprisingly, this work was commissioned by the solemn Spanish court, which Rubens visited in 1603–4.*

‘ *It's the funniest thing you've ever heard*
*I caught a tender little lover*
*Bottom up, rogering his bird,*
*And brandishing my own erection*
*(Venus forgive me!) made a third.* ’

CATULLUS *c.84–54BC*
CATO IT'S LUDICROUS

RIGHT: *In* Stretching Male Torso *of 1986,* **Michael Leonard** *has used pictorial devices that parallel, yet differ from, those used in Wesselmann's female nudes. The head is concealed by the T-shirt that is being langorously removed while the genitals are accentuated by the fact that they too are covered.*

# *All* CHANGE

One of the most important elements in erotic art is not the naked body itself, but the accoutrements with which that body is accompanied and surrounded. Almost any object of clothing, such as a glove or footwear, can become the object of fetishistic fascination. It will not take much inspection of the illustrations included in this book to prove the truth of this observation, nor of the further observation that a degree of concealment focuses erotic feeling in many cases more effectively than the fullest revelation of sexual parts. In addition to this, the partly clothed body is often more erotic in its effect than the entirely naked one. An artist who exploits this fact with great skill is Lucas Cranach, whose numerous versions of *The Judgement of Paris* show the three contending goddesses naked but for unexpected articles of clothing such as a feathered hat. Cranach is also a connoisseur of the erotic effect produced by items of jewellery, especially when these also have metaphoric connotations, a heavy gold chain round the neck of an otherwise nude female, for instance.

Essentially, where the visual image is concerned, there are four ways in which this series of effects can be put to work. The first and simplest is through the retention of some item of ordinary clothing. A woman completely unclothed from the waist down, but fully dressed otherwise, presents a far more erotic image than one who is completely unclothed, simply because attention is immediately directed to what is uncovered. The second comes from the adoption of unusual items of clothing, with fetishistic and ritualistic connotations. The dominatrix's wasp-waisted leather corset, high heels and

' *I went down the steps. Riding crops stood in an umbrella stand. Cat o' nine tails poked out of a wooden barrel. On the wall hung hand cuffs, gags, nipple clamps and penis rings. Steel braces to lock the legs in place. Iron masks that looked like they'd been used in a medieval torture chamber. Condoms in rainbow colours lined the shelves, some with tiger's heads, some shaped like dragons, some that looked like nothing I'd ever seen on earth.* '

CARLA TONEY
MRS BRENTON'S DILDO

whip convey blatant sexual messages. So too do the leatherman's harness and heavy boots. Both of these costumes involve the exaggeration of already existing sexual characteristics. A third involves incongruity – a man in female dress or portions of it, a woman similarly attired. Marlene Dietrich appeared in masculine evening dress, white tie and tails, to enormous erotic effect.

A fourth method is in the hands of the artist rather than that of his subject and involves the skilful cropping and editing of the image. Michael Leonard's *Changing Head*, a painting reproduced in this book, is more sexual and sensual than the majority of male nudes. It is a close-up view of a man's head. He is pulling off a T-shirt, in such a way that his eyes and brow are concealed. The only things which appear clearly are his mouth and the beard surrounding it.

Images of this sort have clearly been influenced by photography, which suggests new methods of composition, where the part substitutes for the whole.

Costume, specialist accoutrements, compositional devices which control what can be seen and how much can be seen, are the business of the visual artist. Descriptions of clothing or the partial absence of it can never be as powerful as actually seeing the thing itself. Nor can any writer, however skilful, control the reader's point of view, in the most literal sense of this term, to anything like the same extent as a painter or a photographer.

The literary form where costume obviously counts for most is the drama, since this is a visual just as much as it is a verbal event. In this connection one has to consider a number of things. The first is the use of the mask, which conceals identity, and which at the same time focuses

'*As soon as I saw her legs, I imagined them coiled or clasped around my neck. She had on a pair of black, patent leather shoes with straps around the ankles, fetishistic heels six inches high and, in all the heat and paranoia of summer, an immense coat of red fox was slung around her shoulders; I will always associate her, with some reason, with foxes. This coat revealed only the hem of a dark blue, white coin-dotted dress that hardly covered her. Her hair was a furze-bush, à la Africain, and she had bright purple lipstick on her mouth. She loitered among the confession magazines, chewing a stick of candy — a Babe Ruth, or some other item of edible Americana, singing a soft, high, vacant, lovely song. There was a drugged smile on her face.*'

ANGELA CARTER *1940–92*
THE PASSION OF NEW EVE 1977

attention on the whole of the body rather than on the features. Blotting out the features in this way turns attention away from the nuances of expression and therefore of personality, and deflects it to the actual physical being. The most erotic of the images of New Orleans prostitutes taken by E. J. Bellocq are undoubtedly those in which the subject is nude but masked.

A more important aspect of the theatre, however, is the tradition of playing roles *in travesti*. This has established itself in many cultures. In the Chinese opera, and in traditional Japanese theatre, female roles are taken by men. In contemporary Japanese popular entertainment, male roles are sometimes assumed by women. Similar customs existed in the West in Shakespeare's time as is well known, female roles – Portia, Cleopatra, Cordelia – were taken by boys. In some of his comedies, *Twelfth Night* in particular, Shakespeare exploits gender confusion to great effect. In the popular English-speaking theatre this tradition has been inherited by pantomime, where the part of the 'hero', *Dick Whittington* for example, is played by an attractive young woman with excellent legs. A similar convention prevails in J. M. Barrie's perennially successful children's play, *Peter Pan*. 'Trouser' or 'breeches' roles, as they are sometimes called, are also still commonplace in the opera house. Sometimes the parts now taken by women were originally intended to be sung by castrati. Very often, however, they were meant, from the very beginning, to be played by females: examples are Cherubino in Mozart's *The Marriage of Figaro*, 1786; the page Oscar in Verdi's *Ballo in Maschera*, 1859; and Octavian in Richard Strauss's *Der Rosenkavalier*, 1911. Any experienced opera-goer can vouch for the effectiveness of these when they are well acted and sung. Cherubino and Octavian are especially interesting cases in point, since in each case the protagonist is an

ABOVE: *Painted in Germany in the aftermath of World War I,* Young Widow *(1922) by* **Richard Ziegler** *(1891–1992) exploits elements of the black clothes of mourning to a perverse erotic effect.*

adolescent just discovering the force of his own sexuality. *Der Rosenkavalier* offers a peculiarly powerful *coup de théâtre*. Before the curtain rises on the first act, the spectator hears voluptuously stormy music which represents a vigorous bout of love-making between the Marschallin and her young lover. When the lovers are revealed to the audience, they are still in bed. It is only with Octavian's first phrases that it becomes apparent that the part has been assigned to a female. This sets an ambiguous but intensely erotic tone for the piece as a whole. It must of course be remembered that it comes from precisely the same cultural milieu as the erotic work of Egon Schiele.

The theme of transvestism has enjoyed enduring popularity in erotic literature. Among its most famous manifestations are Théophile Gautier's novel *Mademoiselle de Maupin* (1835), which Swinburne made the theme of

LEFT: **Egon Schiele** *was a master of poignant eroticism. Here his favourite model,* Wally *Neuzil, retains her stockings and blouse to create a more powerful erotic effect.*

ABOVE: *Working under the pseudonym Don Fletcher,* **David Pearce** *uses sado-masochistic accessories to indicate that this picture of Andy is aimed at a very specialized niche market.*

' *Half a dozen men dressed like avengers from the middle ages...* '

CARLA TONEY
MRS BRENTON'S DILDO

ABOVE: *In his 1987 Self-Portrait,* **John Kirby** *has posed wearing a dress to indicate his uncertain sexual identity.*

an enthusiastic sonnet, in which he speaks of 'the unknown God of unachieved desire', and Virginia Woolf's fantasy *Orlando* (1928), based on her own relationship with the rather masculine Vita Sackville-West.

Clothing and accessories, as ways of projecting a particular view of sexuality, are not stable elements, and this can lead to sudden ironic confrontations between reality and expectation. In his *Autobiography*, Benvenuto Cellini (1500–71) gleefully recounts winning a bet by bringing a youth from his studio to an artists' feast dressed as a woman. No one detected the imposture, and his companion was voted the most beautiful of all.

In the earlier part of the present century, gay men and lesbian women were supposed to signal their sexual preferences not merely by their mannerisms, but by what

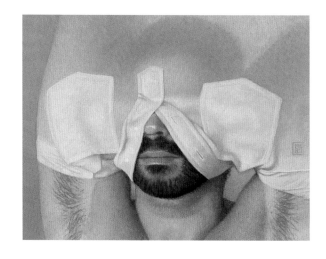

ABOVE: **Michael Leonard's** *intensely erotic* Changing Head *of 1982 uses no primary sexual signifiers.*

*Sexuality is obliquely and powerfully suggested by means of displacement, editing and metaphor.*

they wore. At one time, suede shoes were thought of as a sure sign of male homosexuality. Since 'gay liberation', however, homosexual dress has often favoured exaggeratedly masculine stereotypes. In San Francisco, there were violent protests outside City Hall following the murder the openly gay local politician Harvey Milk. The *San Francisco Chronicle*, reporting these disturbances, remarked that the participants were 'typical homosexuals', with cropped haircuts, clipped moustaches, jeans and checked workshirts. Only ten years earlier, these accoutrements would not have seemed typical at all.

LEFT: *Young Icarus or an angel in flesh? This extraordinary photograph by* **Roberto Rincón** *of 1995 treads the thin line between dressing to thrill and simply dressing up.*

ABOVE: *Closely related to his Great American Nude series,* **Tom Wesselmann**'s *1966 watercolour, Helen, concentrates on primary sexual signifiers.*

*All indicators of individual personality are obscured. The long black stockings, a traditional device also used by Schiele, focuses attention on the pubic area.*

' *the black mesh stockings she wore designated their length and slenderness as specifically erotic; she would not use them to run away with.* '

ANGELA CARTER *1940–92*
THE PASSION OF NEW EVE 1977

Perhaps the most fascinating cases historically have been those in which the fetishization of clothing becomes an integral part of the personality of a particular individual. One of the best-known examples, dating from the eighteenth century, is that of the Chevalier d'Eon, diplomat and spy, who passed most of his life dressed as a lady of fashion.

In some celebrated cases, particularly where females are involved, it is difficult to be sure whether the decision to assume masculine dress was due to inner compulsion or simply to practical necessity. Good examples of this ambiguity would be the female pirates Mary Read and Anne Bonny. The former seems to have felt the attraction of male dress early on. At the beginning of the eighteenth century, she served for seven years as a soldier in Flanders, only dropping her disguise when she fell in love with a comrade. Later, she reverted to masculine costume and became successively a seaman, a privateer and a pirate.

She was eventually captured on the same ship as Anne Bonny, the illegitimate daughter of a Cork lawyer who settled with his mistress at Charleston, South Carolina. Bonny eloped with a dashing pirate captain, one Jack Rackham, and it was while she was serving on his ship that justice caught up with her and the rest of the crew off the coast of Jamaica. Read and Bonny are reported to have fought bravely, while the male members of the crew, including Rackham, fled and took refuge in the hold. At the subsequent trial, the two women managed to escape the gallows by 'pleading their bellies', that is, by announcing that they were both with child. This argues that their orientation was primarily heterosexual. Anne was nevertheless a tough individual. When Rackham, on

1. Jules Quicherat, *Procès de Condamnation de Jeanne d'Arc*, 5 vols (Paris 1841–9) Vol II p. 439.

2. ibid, pp. 402 and 433.

3. Pierre Tissot and Yvonne Lanhers. *Procès de Condamnation de Jeanne d'Arc*, 3 vols (Paris 1960–71) Vol I, p. 128; Vol II p. 15.

the day of his execution, was brought to take his farewell, she turned from him, saying coldly, 'that she was sorry to see him there, but if he had fought like a man, he need not have been hanged like a dog'.

An even more celebrated case is that of Joan of Arc (1412–31). Joan's decision to put on masculine attire is integral to the whole of her extraordinary story, and it was her insistence on resuming it which precipitated her end. At Joan's trial in Rouen, her clothes provided the subject-matter for more than one question. Responding to these, Joan was always stubborn, and often evasive. Asked who had ordered her to put on men's clothing, she replied: 'It is a little thing and of small importance. I did not don it by the advice of the men of this world; I donned it only by

BELOW: *In this fantasy by leading nineteenth-century erotic artist* **Félicien Rops** (1855–98), *the revealing yet constrictive costume worn by* Woman on a Rocking Horse *is an intrinsic part of her allure.*

command of God and the angels.' [1] Her mode of dress meant so much to her that she even refused to change it in order to hear mass and take communion.

Anyone familiar with modern psychoanalytic ways of thinking would conclude that this sounds like an inner compulsion at work, and that similar compulsions have motivated other, more modern transvestites. Yet it must also be noted that Joan's change of dress was, in her case, a means of taking on a new social as well as a new sexual identity. Very soon after she arrived at the court of Charles VII of France, we hear of her dressed in the manner of a young nobleman in 'very noble cloth of gold and silk with much fur'. [2] This description is confirmed by several of the articles of accusation presented to Joan at her trial. One mentions that she was captured wearing 'a gold huque, open on every side'. [3] A huque was a kind of surcoat, with floating panels of cloth. Made of velours vermeil, as yet another source tells us, it must have been a splendid garment indeed. It is noticeable that, at her trial, Joan scarcely bothered to challenge the descriptions that were given of her dress.

Throughout her career Joan placed great emphasis on the notion of hierarchy, of everything being in its proper place and every individual knowing what category he belonged to, and behaving according to the rules of that category. On the other hand, she always claimed that she herself was exceptional, because she had been chosen by God for her mission. Her clothes, their richness as well as their masculinity, were a way of making the difference visible. They were a silent but conspicuous assertion of her claim to be someone to whom no common rules applied. Born a peasant and a woman, she transformed herself into a prince and a man.

Yet clearly her actions in this respect were not simply part of a rational campaign of propaganda. Though she presented herself as asexual, they look very much like the appearance, in transmuted guise, of impulses which were at their roots profoundly sexual. Clothing and accessories speak for sex. When we transpose or exaggerate them, we speak about our own sexual natures.

RIGHT: *The rape and subsequent suicide of Roman heroine Lucretia gave artists a chance to combine the notions of sex and violence. This depiction of the unfortunate Lucretia was painted in the early sixteenth century by* **The Master of the Holy Blood** *(op. c.1520.)*

# *Love* HURTS

*t*he combination of pain and pleasure in eroticism is universally acknowledged and almost as universally courted and feared. Its roots seem to be planted extremely deeply within the human psyche. One specific difficulty is that when pain and sex combine they often present themselves in religious terms. One does not have to search very far in the Judaeo-Christian tradition to find proof of this, though the same combination occurs in other religions as well. Any student of Christian iconography, for example, comes to understand that the growing command exercised by artists over realistic presentation of the human figure was in part at least prompted by a desire to make the sufferings of Christ and the saints more vivid to the worshipper, and that, additionally, that this immediacy of presentation was meant to lead to direct, empathetic identification with the torments portrayed.

In developing their art in this way, Renaissance artists were able to find hints in the surviving art of antiquity. The works which especially influenced them tended to be originals or copies from the Hellenistic period, which was the first to put so much stress on representations of the human body as a vehicle for emotional expression. Sculptures such as the *Dying Gaul* and the *Laocoon* suggest that pain and struggle undoubtedly have a sexual component. The chief figure of the *Laocoon* group, if one saw the head alone, might easily be mistaken for a representation of a man in the throes of orgasm.

From the late fifteenth century onwards Christian artists produced religious masterpieces whose sexual component could hardly be disguised. Early examples are

' *Lady, you think you spite me*
*When by the lip you bite me,*
*But if you think it trouble*
*Then let my pain be double -*
*Aye, triple! – but you bliss me,*
*For though you bite, you kiss me*
*And with sour sweet delight me.* '

ANON
LADY, YOU THINK YOU SPITE ME

Mantegna's heroic *St Sebastian* in the Ca' d'Oro in Venice, and Sebastiano del Piombo's *Martyrdom of St Agatha* in the Galleria Pitti in Florence. It is significant that, in both cases, the holy legend depicted already had a strongly sexual component. It has been suggested, for instance, that the tale of St Sebastian being shot full of arrows is in fact an allegory of his multiple rape by the Roman soldiery. In Piombo's painting, a voluptuous, nearly nude St Agatha is having her nipples tweaked with red-hot pincers, as a preliminary to her final martyrdom.

Both these paintings belong to a period before the rise of the Counter-Reformation. St Ignatius of Loyola, one of the chief figures in this movement to rescue and reform a church badly shaken by the rise of Protestantism, in his *Spiritual Exercises* encouraged his followers to identify as closely as possible with the physical sufferings of Christ. This had a marked impact on the development of art. Baroque artists used every technical device to make the spectator not merely a witness of, but an actual sharer in, the torments depicted.

LVCRECIÆ · ROMANÆ

BELOW: *The allegorical themes of* Le Temps enchaînant la beauté *(Time Enslaves Beauty)* enabled Venetian painter **Pietro Liberi** *(1614–87) to hint at more recondite kinky sexual activites.*

' *Follow, follow*
*Through with mischief*
*Armed, like whirlwind*
*Now she flies thee;*
*Time can conquer*
*Love's unkindness;*
*Love can alter*
*Time's disgraces;*
*Till death faint not*
*Then but follow.*
*Could I catch that*
*Nimble traitor,*
*Scornful Laura,*
*Swiftfoot Laura,*
*Soon then would I*
*Seek avengement.*
*What's th'avangement?*
*Even submissely*
*Prostrate then to*
*Beg for mercy.* '

THOMAS CAMPION
*1567–1620*
OBSERVATIONS IN THE ART
OF ENGLISH POESY, 1602

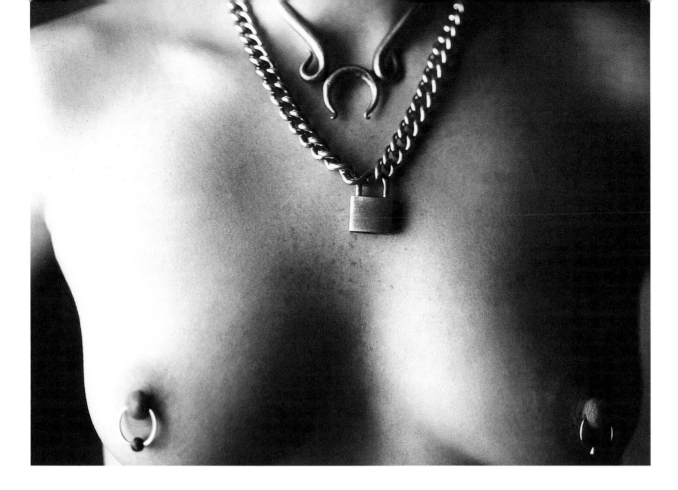

ABOVE: **Donna Day**'s depiction of a woman with pierced nipples is a blatant reference to sado-masochism. Body piercing and symbolic jewellery such as chains and padlocks are frequently used as symbols to show that the wearer has SM sexual preferences.

The mixture of religious ecstasy and something which seems much more specifically sexual also recurs in the writings of the great religious mystics of the Counter-Reformation period – most notably of all, perhaps, in those of Loyola's fellow-Spaniard, St Teresa of Avila. In a famous passage in her autobiography Teresa describes an angelic vision:

'But it was our Lord's will that I should see this angel in the following way. He was not tall but short, and very beautiful; and his face was so aflame that he appeared to be one of the highest rank of angels, who seem to be all on fire... In his hands I saw a great golden spear, and at the iron tip there appeared to be a point of fire. This he plunged into my heart several times so that it penetrated my entrails. When he pulled it out, I felt that he took them with it, and left me utterly consumed by the great love of God. '[1]

Gianlorenzo Bernini (1598–1680), the leading sculptor of the Roman Baroque, used this image as the subject of his *Altar of St Teresa* of 1645, which forms part of the Cornaro Chapel in Santa Maria della Vittoria in Rome. Here the saint swoons in response to the angel's assault in a manner which strikes modern spectators as erotic.

The formulae invented by Renaissance and Baroque artists for the exploration of religious themes continue to be adapted to modern usages. In the late 1950s and 1960s, for example, there was a fashion for so-called 'peplum movies' about the adventures of Hercules and other Greek and Roman super-heroes. The best known of these was *Hercules Unchained* (1958), which featured the American bodybuilding champion Steve Reeves. In this and other similar parts Reeves remarkable musculature was cannily displayed by showing him tied up or chained up in various ingenious ways. In such scenes he was a direct successor of St Sebastian and the other victims listed in Christian martyrology, and part of the audience certainly derived an erotic thrill from the predicaments in which he found himself.

1. *The Life of St. Teresa of Avila, by Herself*, translated by J. M. Cohen (Penguin Classics, 1957).

ABOVE: *Gay artist* **Delmas Howe** *here equates the Stations of the Cross with gay sado-masochism. The setting of The Flagellation is a pier on the West Side of New York, a scene of much homosexual activity in the 1970s before AIDS.*

Despite this, one surprising feature of these peplum movies, granted their late date, is their apparent innocence, and lack of awareness of the sexual messages they convey. The idea of pain for pleasure's sake was not unknown to the writers as well as the artists of the sixteenth and seventeenth centuries. Thomas Otway's seventeenth-century play features a lecherous Venetian senator who enjoys being flagellated, and accounts of eighteenth-century brothels in London make it clear that sound whippings, both given and received, were modes of enjoyment which they regularly purveyed to a demanding clientele.

However, it was not perhaps until the appearance on the scene of the Marquis de Sade that a more elaborate analysis was made of the sado-masochistic impulse. Sade's novels, published in the relatively brief interval between his release from a long imprisonment at the outbreak of the French Revolution and his re-incarceration under Napoleon, were by far the most elaborate fantasies of their type ever to reach even a restricted public.

They set the tone for an exploration of such material which lasted throughout the nineteenth century, and which continues into the present. These researches gradually became coloured by the theories and discoveries of Freud. Two things took place. Mainstream literature and art gradually became more interested in making use of such material; and supposedly 'underground' texts which dealt with it acquired a kind of intellectual respectability which had never previously been accorded to them.

One of the most important literary texts in which an interest in this kind of activity gradually makes itself felt is Marcel Proust's great *roman fleuve, A la Recherche du Temps Perdu*. Written from 1913 until his death in 1922. Proust's study of homosexual sado-masochism is conducted through the analysis of one of the major characters in the novel, the Baron de Charlus. In the last volume the narrator stumbles into a brothel one wartime evening in Paris, and comes across Charlus who has come there as a client:

ABOVE: *In this* Untitled *piece from 1978, Colombian artist* **Luis Caballero** *(1943–95) combines explicit newspaper photographic images of murders with implicit intimations of homosexual violence.*

' Suddenly from a room situated by itself at the end of a corridor, I thought I heard stifled groans. I walked rapidly towards the sounds and put my ear to the door. "I beseech you, mercy, have pity, untie me, don't beat me so hard," said a voice. "I kiss your feet, I abase myself, I promise not to offend again. Have pity on me." "No, you filthy brute," replied another voice, "and if you yell and drag yourself about on your knees like that, you'll be tied to the bed, no mercy for you," and I heard the noise of the crack of a whip, which I guessed to be reinforced with nails, for it was followed by cries of pain. At this moment I noticed that there was a small oval window opening from the room on to the corridor and that the curtain had not been drawn across it; stealthily in the darkness I crept as far as this window and there in the room, chained to the bed like Prometheus to his rock, receiving the blows that Maurice rained upon him with a whip which was in fact studded with nails, I saw, with blood already flowing from him and covered with bruises which proved that chastisement was not taking place for the first time – I saw before me M de Charlus. '[2]

2. Marcel Proust, *In Search of Lost Time: Volume 6, Time Regained*, translated by Andreas Mayor and Terence Kilmartin, revised by D. J. Enright (Vintage, London, 1996) p. 154.

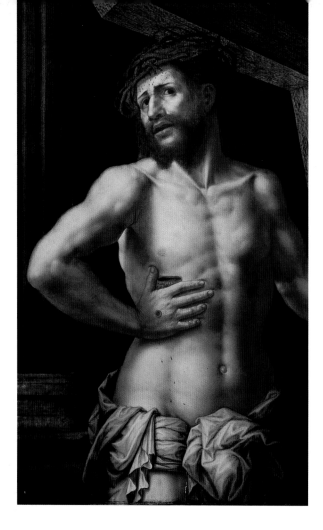

ABOVE: *In* Le Christ de Douleurs Montrant ses Plaies, **Jan Sanders van Hemessen** *(1519–60)* *shows how scenes of martyrdoms and passion frequently cross the boundaries of erotica.*

In France, especially, the exploration of 'extreme' sexual material became a twentieth-century fashion. It played a prominent part in the imagery of the Surrealist Movement, most prominently of all in the work of Dalí and of Hans Bellmer, and it spawned at least one novel of great literary elegance, *The Story of O*. Always attributed to a female author, Pauline Réage, otherwise unknown, this is now generally understood to be the work of the great stylist Jean Paulhan, editor of the *Nouvelle Revue Française*, whose name appears on the cover only as the author of a long afterword.

First published in 1954, *The Story of O* follows the pattern of a number of Victorian pornographic novels – at that epoch these texts were more usually English than French – in describing female rather than male

submission and humiliation. As part of a sequence of dream-like events the central character O is first borne away by her lover René to a mysterious country house where she is 'trained'. Then she is handed over to his older half-brother, the Englishman Sir Stephen:

' "Kneel down, I have something to say to you," he said. "I'm afraid René has prepared you very poorly." "I always obey René," she stammered. "You fail to distinguish between love and obedience. You're going to obey me without loving me and without my loving you." Thereupon he felt a storm of revolt rise in her, a storm of the strangest revolt, silently and within her denying the words she had heard, denying the promises of submission and slavery she'd given, denying her own consent, her own desire, her nakedness, her sweat, her trembling legs, the circles round her eyes. She ground her teeth and fought when, having whirled behind her, bent her spine forward until her elbows and forehead touched the floor, jammed his thighs behind hers and forced up her haunches, he drove himself into her anus, tearing her as René had said she would be glad to have him do. The first time, she did not scream. He went more brutally to work, and she screamed. And every time he withdrew, then plunged in again, every time, hence, that he wanted her to, she screamed. She screamed from loathing and revulsion as much as from pain, and he knew it. She knew it too, and knowing it was the measure of her defeat, she knew she was beaten and that it pleased him to force her to scream. '[3]

The literary and artistic examples I have chosen here all focus on the submission of the masochist, and this is perhaps to offer a false impression of this category of erotica. There is almost as much which focuses on the figure of the master or dominatrix. The latter figures in one of her milder incarnations in yet another Victorian erotic novel, *First Training*, which describes how a stepmother trains her stepdaughters to become accomplished dominatrixes. It is one of the daughters who tells the story:

' "Smithers!" I called, for such as his surname and instinct told me not to address him at this moment by other than such. The door opened immediately and he stood there, then hesitated and entered, closing the door quietly as might a footman. I held my head high although in truth I quivered inwardly. Standing to attention, his head bowed, he waited.

**3**. Pauline Réage, *The Story of O*, (Corgi Books, London, 1972) p. 120.

ABOVE: Caught Smoking, 1994, is by Los Angeles photographer/film director **Rick Castro**, who specializes in images of hustlers.

'*Even submissely Prostrate then to Beg for mercy.*'

"Here!" I all but barked and pointed to the floor immediately in front of me. Not meeting my eyes, he came forward and the silence about us seemed tremendous. "Kneel! Kneel and lick my shoes!" I said, keeping with great effort a quavering from my voice.

He obeyed on the instant, his nose first scraping the ground and his back bowed. Raising my skirt no more than was necessary, he uncovered my buckled shoes and impressed his lips upon the toes of them fervently, one after the other. It tickled a little through the leather, but I liked it. I knew my stance, my high station. I had reached, as it seemed to me, the very summit of female ambitions. His mouth brushed back and forth with the submissiveness of a trained dog.

"Go!" I said coldly and therewith, without the faintest protest or raising of his eyes to mine, he lumbered up and retreated, not wiping his lips as I fleetingly thought he might, for that would have been a sign of gross rebellion and discourtesy. Indeed his tongue flicked quickly about his mouth as though the very taste of the dust on my shoes pleased him. Then he was gone, the door closing soundlessly once more, and immediately after my stepmother entered and drew me lovingly into her arms. "My little conqueror!" she crooned and it was then as if the gates of life had opened wide to me and I waited upon our new adventures. '[4]

As with all Victorian erotica, it must be remembered that this is a text almost certainly written by a man, and quite certainly addressed to a male audience.

ABOVE: *American-based Japanese artist* **Masami Teraoka** *revives aspects of* the ukiyo-e *tradition in his* 1989 Study for Australia series/Ayers Rock Fantasy.

The whole subject of sado-masochistic fantasy is a peculiarly difficult one today, since our perceptions of eroticism and how it functions seem to have narrowed at least as much in some areas as they have apparently widened in others. As a friend wrote to me recently:

*' We have established these strange equations in our society: Love = Sex; Innocence = lack of sexual knowledge; Loss of innocence = loss of virginity. Very peculiar when our society is so saturated with sexual imagery. '*

188    4. Anonymous, *First Training* (Wordsworth Editions, Ware, Hertfordshire, 1996) pp. 105–6.

The literalism of contemporary attitudes makes such fantasies seem peculiarly threatening, and at the same time restores to them an allure which they had once seemed in danger of losing in a climate which was supposedly more and more 'permissive'. In fact, the nature of what is and what is not transgressive shifts every time one examines the subject. If one looks, for example, at a subject to which I have deliberately refrained from giving any space in this book, that of eroticism and children, the state of contemporary opinion is in some ways substantially less, not more, judgmental than it was in the nineteenth century. The whole question of child sexuality is one which makes a large section of the contemporary audience feel intensely threatened. Rousseau and Freud between them have a great deal to answer for. Even apart from this, erotic imagery – both literary and visual – continues to trouble the intellect, the imagination and even the dreams of contemporary society. It can safely be said that no other general category of imagery has an equivalent power. And none takes us so directly to the sources of human personality and indeed to the sources of life itself.

LEFT: Woman at a Balcony (1988) by **Masami Teraoka**, executed in the traditional Japanese style yet dotted with contemporary western ephemera: sunglasses, prophylactics. Is the western man really hurting his eastern partner, or is this just the clash of cultures?

'*I squeezed and pressed into his flesh with my fingers, my teeth sinking as deeply into his shoulder as I dared without drawing blood.*'

UNSIGNED
FROM PLEASURES: WOMEN WRITE EROTICA
EDITED BY LONNIE BARBACH, 1984

# Index of artists

Figures in *italics* refer to illustrations.

## ACKNOWLEDGEMENTS

The publishers wish to thank the following for the use of pictures:

Albertina Graphic Collection, Vienna/Bridgeman Art Library: p. 38
Bruce Ayres/Tony Stone Images: p. 48
Michael Ayrton (private collection): p. 107
Don Bachardy/Lizardi Harp Gallery: pp. 27, 30, 32, 33
Bonham's, London/Bridgeman Art Library: pp. 29, 135
Bridgeman Art Library: pp. 12, 18, 76, 78-9(C), 96, 111, 127, 142, 157, 161, 165
British Library/Bridgeman Art Library: pp. 67, 156
British Museum/Bridgeman Art Library: pp. 43, 179
Bruce of Los Angeles, private collection, London: p. 26
Budapest Museum of Fine Arts/Bridgeman Art Library: p. 125
Tony Butcher, Adonis Art, London: pp. 25, 31
Rick Castro/courtesy Wessel/O'Connor Gallery: p. 187
Judy Chicago, Through the Flower, Belen, New Mexico: p. 82(T and B)
Christie's, London/Bridgeman Art Library: pp. 2, 21, 35, 62, 97
Ricardo Cinalli, Beaux Arts Gallery, London: p. 152
Francesco Clemente/Thomas Ammon Fine Art AG: p. 47
Timothy Cummings/Catherine Clark Gallery: p. 140
Donna Day/Tony Stone Images: p. 183
Galleria Degli, Offizi, Florence/Bridgeman Art Library: p. 119
Antonia Deutsch/Tony Stone Images: p. 15
Dinodia/Trip: p. 83
Nick Dolding/Tony Stone Images: p. 7
Wei Dong, Hanart TZ, Hong Kong: pp. 137, 167
He Douling, Hanart TZ, Hong Kong: p. 102
George Dureau, artist (private collection): pp. 23, 116
Mary Evans Picture Library: p. 45
Eric Fisch/Thomas Amman Fine Art AG: p. 112
Fogg Art Museum/Bridgeman Art Library: p. 101
Jack Fritscher, photographer: pp. 103, 107
Jean François Gate/Tony Stone Images: pp. 53, 158
Eric Gill: pp. 24, 85
Giraudon/Bridgeman Art Library: pp. 52, 59, 71
Claude Guillarmin/Tony Stone Images: p. 81
David Hanover/Tony Stone Images: p. 45
Frank Herholdt/Tony Stone Images: p. 40
David Hockney/ © D. Hockney 1983: p. 16
Harry Holland/Jill George Gallery: p.115
Delmas Howe, Rio Bravo Fine Art, Truth-or-Consequences, New Mexico: pp. 144, 184
Index/Bridgeman Art Library: p. 55
Rod Judkins, private collection, London: p. 110
John Kirby, Flowers, East London: p. 175
Lisa Kokin/Catharine Clark Gallery: p. 121
Kunsthistorisches Museum, Vienna/Bridgeman Art Library: p. 104
Lady Lever Art Gallery/Bridgeman Art Library: p. 41
Michael Leonard, artist: pp. 170(T), 176(T), 178
The Louvre/Bridgeman Art Library: p. 147
Victor Lownes Collection, London/Bridgeman Art Library: p. 163
Edward Lucie-Smith: pp. 10, 108, 109
Stefan May/Tony Stone Images: pp. 50, 74, 80
Josef Mensing Gallery/Bridgeman Art Library: p. 131
Chris Nelson, photographer: pp. 19, 113, 117
Nezu Art Museum, Tokyo/Bridgeman Art Library: p. 166
Gerard Nordman, Geneva/Bridgeman Art Library: p. 129
Erik Olson/Lizardi Harp Gallery: p. 22
Pablo Picasso/Thomas Amman Fine Art AG: p. 122
David Pearce, artist: p. 174

Yu Peng, Hanart TZ, Hong Kong: p. 91
Prado, Madrid/Bridgeman Art Library: pp. 8, 105, 108-69
Pushkin Museum/Bridgeman Art Library: p. 63
Lorne Resnick/Tony Stone Images: p. 44
Roberto Rincon (photographer): p. 176(B)
Zsuzsi Roboz/David Messum Fine Art: p. 75
Andrew Rodney/Tony Stone Images: p. 51
Stephanie Rushton/Tony Stone Images: p. 39
Jean Rustin, Jean Rustin Foundation, Antwerp: p. 149
Andres Serrano, the Groningen Museum: pp. 15(T), 153
Elke Selzle/Tony Stone Images: p. 89
Scott Siedman/Catharine Clark Gallery: pp. 64, 68, 69, 70
Stapleton Collection/Bridgeman Art Library: pp. 87, 123, 162, 164
Masami Teraoka/Catharine Clark Gallery: pp. 146, 189
Jerome Tisne/Tony Stone Images: p. 49
Arthur Tress/Stephen Cohen Gallery: pp. 17, 151
Keith Vaughan, artist, private collection, London: p. 79
National Gallery of Victoria, Melbourne/Bridgeman Art Library: p. 100
Victoria & Albert Museum/Bridgeman Art Library: p. 84
Visual Arts Library: pp. 6, 9, 13, 37, 42, 54, 57, 58, 61, 65, 66, 73, 77, 79, 86, 90, 92, 98, 99, 120, 124, 126, 128, 132, 134, 136, 138, 143, 145, 151, 154, 155, 172, 173, 181, 182, 185, 186 189
Wallace Collection/Bridgeman Art Library: p. 141
Wartenberg/Zefa: pp. 14, 88
Liu Wei, Hanart TZ, Hong Kong: p. 46
Tom Wesselman/Thomas Amman Fine Art AG: p. 177
Peter Willi/Bridgeman Art Library: p. 16(B)
Evelyn Williams, artist and City Art Galleries, Manchester: p. 93

The publishers gratefully acknowledge permission to reproduce the following material in this book:

p. 8 *Let's fuck, dear heart* by Pietro Aretino translated by Alistair Elliot by permission of Macmillan Publishers.

p. 20 From *The Swimming Pool Library* by Alan Hollinghurst © 1988 Alan Hollinghurst, reprinted with the permission of Chatto & Windus, and with the permission of Aitken & Stone Ltd.

p. 25 *The Wingless & The Winged* from *Making Love* by Erica Jong. Reprinted by permission of Sterling Lord Literistic, Inc. Copyright © 1978 by Erica Jong.

p. 30 From *The Swimming Pool Library* by Alan Hollinghurst © 1988 Alan Hollinghurst, reprinted with the permission of Chatto & Windus, and with the permission of Aitken & Stone Ltd.

p. 38 From *The Kindness of Women* by J. G. Ballard by permission of HarperCollins.

p. 47 *The Long Tunnel of Wanting You* from *Making Love* by Erica Jong. Reprinted by permission of Sterling Lord Literistic, Inc. Copyright © 1978 by Erica Jong.

p. 48 From *Mediaeval Latin Lyrics* translated by Helen Waddell by permission of Constable & Co. Copyright © Helen Waddell, 1929.

p. 54 From *Neruda: Selected Poems* by Pablo Neruda, edited by Nathaniel Tarn by permission of Jonathan Cape.

p. 61 From *The Erotic Poems* by Ovid, translated by Peter Green (Penguin Classics, 1982). Copyright © Peter Green, 1982.

p. 78 From *In the Cut* by Susanna Moore by permission of Random House.

p. 82 *she being Brand* by e.e.cummings by permission of HarperCollins.

p. 84 From *Portnoy's Complaint* by Philip Roth by permission of Jonathan Cape.

p. 94 *Miss Twye* from *Collected Poems 1980–1990* by Gavin Ewart by permission of Hutchinson and the Estate of Gavin Ewart.

p. 96 From *The Woman on the Dunes* by Anaïs Nin by permission of Penguin Books Ltd.

p. 102 From *The Woman on the Dunes* by Anaïs Nin by permission of Penguin Books Ltd.

p. 117 From *A Matter of Life and Sex* by Oscar Moore by permission of Penguin Books Ltd.

p. 120 From *The Metamorphoses of Ovid* translated by Mary M. Innes (Penguin Classics, 1955). Copyright © Mary M. Innes, 1995.

p. 120 *Oppenheim's Cup and Saucer* is taken from *Standing Female Nude* by Carol Ann Duffy published by Anvil Press Poetry in 1985.

p. 126 *Sappho, IX* by permission of the translator Terence DuQuesne.

p. 127 From *Mothers and Other Lovers* by Joanna Briscoe by permission of Phoenix House.

p. 128 From *The High Cost of Living* by Marge Piercy, published in Great Britain by The Women's Press Ltd, 1979, 34 Great Sutton Street, London EC1V 0DX. Used by permission of The Women's Press Ltd. Copyright © 1978 by Marge Piercy and Middlemarsh, Inc. Reprinted by permission of the Wallace Literary Agency, Inc.

p. 137 From *The Blue Afternoon* by William Boyd by permission of Penguin Books Ltd.

p. 142 Quotation by Bharthabi, translated by John Brough, by permission of Penguin Books Ltd.

p. 148 From *Dildoes* by Fiona Pitt-Kethley by permission of the author.

p. 157 *The Jokes of Early Aviation* from *Collected Poems 1980–1990* by Gavin Ewart by permission of Hutchinson and the Estate of Gavin Ewart.

p. 160 From *Pleasures: Women Write Erotica*, edited by Lonnie Barbach by permission of Weidenfeld & Nicolson.

p. 165 From *Elena* by Anaïs Nin by permission of Penguin Books Ltd.

p. 167 *Mia's Fantasy* from *Women on Top* by Nancy Friday by permission of Hutchinson.

p. 169 From *Cato it's Ludicrous* translated by James Michie by permission of Pan Macmillan.

p. 170 From *Mrs Brenton's Dildo* © Carla Toney, from *Backrubs*, 1996 reprinted by permission of Serpent's Tail, London.

p. 172 From *The Passion of New Eve* by Angela Carter. Copyright © Angela Carter. Reproduced by permission of the Estate of Angela Carter c/o Rogers, Coleridge & White Ltd, 20 Powis Mews, London W11 1JN and Virago Press.

p. 174 From *Mrs Brenton's Dildo* © Carla Toney, from *Backrubs*, 1996 reprinted by permission of Serpent's Tail, London.

p. 177 From *The Passion of New Eve* by Angela Carter. Copyright © Angela Carter. Reproduced by permission of the Estate of Angela Carter c/o Rogers, Coleridge & White Ltd, 20 Powis Mews, London W11 1JN and Virago Press.

p. 189 From *Pleasures: Women Write Erotica*, edited by Lonnie Barbach by permission of Weidenfeld & Nicolson.

Every effort has been made to trace all copyright holders and obtain permissions. The editor and publishers sincerely apologise for any inadvertent errors or omissions and will be happy to correct them in any future editions.